cook's library
Baking

cook's library
Baking

This is a Parragon Publishing Book
This edition published in 2004

Parragon Publishing
Queen Street House
4 Queen Street
Bath BA1 1HE, UK

ISBN: 0-75259-443-5

Printed in China

NOTE

Cup measurements in this book are for American cups. This book
uses imperial and metric measurements. Follow the same units of
measurement throughout; do not mix imperial and metric. All spoon
measurements are level: teaspoons are assumed to be 5 ml,
and tablespoons are assumed to be 15 ml. Unless otherwise stated,
milk is assumed to be full fat, eggs and individual vegetables such
as potatoes are medium, and pepper is freshly ground black pepper.

The times given for each recipe are an approximate guide only because
the preparation times may differ according to the techniques used by
different people and the cooking times may vary as a result of the type
of oven used. The preparation times include chilling and marinating
times, where appropriate.

Recipes using raw or very lightly cooked eggs should be avoided
by infants, the elderly, pregnant women, convalescents, and anyone
suffering from an illness.

Contents

Introduction

It may be a daunting prospect to cook your own savory bakes, tarts, breads, and cakes instead of buying them at the supermarket, but once you have acquired the basic skills—and armed yourself with a few of the "tricks"—it becomes fun, versatile, and rewarding.

There are a few points that will ensure your baking session is successful, regardless of the type of recipe you have chosen. So, before you start:

- Read through the recipe carefully, and make sure you have the right ingredients—using all-purpose flour when self-rising flour is specified, for example, may not produce the result you were expecting!

- Remember to preheat the oven to the required temperature.

- Make sure that you are using the correct size and shape of pan or dish, because the quantities given in the recipe are for the size of the pan specified.

- Prepare the cookware before you start assembling the ingredients— grease or line pans, dishes, or cookie sheets as directed in the recipe.

- Measure the ingredients accurately, and do any basic preparation, such as chopping, slicing, or grating, before you start cooking.

- Once you start cooking, follow the recipe step-by-step, in the order given. Using high-quality ingredients will give the best results— unbleached flours and unrefined sugars are readily available for baking, while fresh vegetables, fish, and good-quality meat from a reliable supplier, and a good, extra virgin olive oil will make all the difference to your savory bakes.

Pie Dough

- Metal pans, not porcelain dishes, are best for quiches and pies.
- Use fat at room temperature, cut into small pieces.
- Use ice water for mixing.
- Pie dough benefits from cool ingredients, and cold hands.
- Always sift the dry ingredients into a large mixing bowl, to incorporate air.
- Wrap the dough in foil and allow it to "rest" in the refrigerator for 30 minutes before using.

Bread

- Plan ahead—most bread recipes include one or two "provings" (leaving the dough in a warm place to double its bulk).
- If the flour feels quite cool, warm it gently in an oven at a low temperature.
- Make sure the liquid is lukewarm, to activate the yeast.
- To knead dough, stretch it away from you with one hand while pulling it toward you with the other, then fold in the edges, give it a quarter turn, and repeat.
- To test whether bread is cooked, tap the base—it should sound hollow if it is done.

Cakes

- Using a loose-bottom pan will make it easier to turn out any type of cake.
- Bring all the ingredients to room temperature before assembling.
- If possible, use a hand-held electric mixer for "creaming" (beating the butter and sugar together until the mixture has a "soft dropping" consistency).
- "Fold in" the dry ingredients very gently, using a metal spoon or spatula in a figure-eight movement. This lets the air get to the mixture and stops the cake becoming too heavy.
- When the cake is cooked, it should feel springy when pressed lightly. Alternatively, when a toothpick is inserted into the center of the cake, it should come out clean if the cake is done.

Traditional Cooking

Trends in eating have changed enormously in recent years to fit in with a greater awareness of health and a busier lifestyle, becoming lighter, healthier, and far more cosmopolitan. But one tradition has survived— the British afternoon tea—which many people still enjoy today. Although it is often restricted to rest days and holidays, the aroma of freshly baked biscuits, muffins, cookies, teabreads, and cakes is as enticing as ever.

Teatime enthusiasts can progress through the year enjoying treats made with seasonal ingredients. Dark winter evenings may be cheered by a deliciously moist Banana and Date Loaf; homemade Teacakes, crammed with dried fruit and glazed with honey, served toasted, perhaps over a log fire; or a rich buttery Clementine Cake, served with coffee or tea.

Later in the year, the arrival of summer is celebrated by a leisurely tea in the garden. Cherry Biscuits, still warm from the oven, might be followed by Strawberry Roulade, a light sponge with a fruity mascarpone cheese filling, topped with toasted almonds and dusted with confectioners' sugar.

The onset of the cooler fall days is lightened by the year's harvest. A glut of apples can be turned into a Spiced Apple Ring, or Crispy-Topped Fruit Bake —an easy-to-make cake decorated with apple slices—while the addition of roasted pumpkin flesh to a recipe makes an unusual and flavorsome Pumpkin Loaf. At any time of year, the tea table can be enhanced by a plate of crisp, melting Shortbread Fantails, or one of the many fruitcake recipes—surely a good reason to start baking.

Equally appetizing, but in a totally different way, are the baking aromas that float from the kitchen of an Italian cook. Here, pasta—in the form of lasagna, cannelloni, or any of the wide variety of shapes—is often served mixed with a sauce of vegetables, fish, or meat, topped with cheese and baked until golden. Spinach and Mushroom Lasagna, Pasticcio, and Shrimp Pasta Bake are just a few examples. Homemade bread is flavored with olives, herbs, cheese, bell peppers, or sun-dried tomatoes, and, of course, garlic is a favorite ingredient in many recipes.

From Italy, too, comes that universal favorite, pizza, said to have been created in Naples. A dough base, spread with a tomato sauce slowly reduced until thick, is topped with a mixture of vegetables and perhaps some Italian sausage, deliciously stringy mozzarella cheese, olives, anchovies, a sprinkling of herbs, and a drizzle of olive oil—the possible combinations are endless, and the end results are wonderful. There are plenty of recipes to choose from such as the classic Pizza Margherita or a delicious Onion, Ham, and Cheese Pizza.

The basic recipe for risotto, a versatile Italian rice dish, can be combined with vegetables and cheese, bound with eggs, and baked to make dishes such as Green Easter Pie.

To round off their meals, Italian cooks often make use of cream and soft, creamy cheeses in desserts, as in the fresh Lemon Mascarpone Cheesecake, which is studded with preserved ginger, or the Tuscan Pudding, which is delicious served with cream.

Basic Recipes

These recipes form the basis of several of the dishes contained in this book. Many of these basic recipes can be made in advance and stored in the refrigerator until required.

Savory Pastry

MAKES 1 x 8-inch/20-cm tart base

1½ cups all-purpose flour, plus extra
    for dusting
pinch of salt
6 tbsp butter, plus extra for greasing
2–3 tbsp water

1 Mix the flour and salt together in a bowl. Rub in the butter, then add the water and mix to form a soft dough. Wrap in plastic wrap and let chill for 30 minutes.

2 Grease an 8-inch/20-cm tart pan. Roll out the dough on a floured surface and use to line the pan. Prick the dough with a fork, then cover and let chill for 30 minutes.

3 Line the pie shell with foil and fill with baking beans. Bake in a preheated oven, 400°F/200°C, for 10–12 minutes until golden. Remove from the oven, discard the baking beans and foil, then bake in the oven for another 10 minutes.

4 Remove from the oven, then add you chosen filling and cook as in main recipe.

Sweet Pastry

MAKES 1 x 9½-inch/24-cm tart base

1½ cups all-purpose flour, plus extra
    for dusting
1 oz/25 g superfine sugar
½ cup butter, plus extra for greasing
1 tbsp water

1 Mix the flour and sugar together in a bowl. Rub in the butter, then add the water and mix to form a soft dough. Wrap in plastic wrap and let chill for 30 minutes.

2 Grease a 9½-inch/24-cm tart pan. Roll out the dough on a lightly floured surface and use to line the pan. Prick the dough with a fork, then cover with plastic wrap and let chill again for 30 minutes.

3 Line the pie shell with foil and fill with baking beans. Bake in a preheated oven, 375°F/190°C for 15 minutes. Remove from the oven discard the baking beans and foil, then bake for another 15 minutes.

4 Remove from the oven, then add your chosen filling and cook as in main recipe.

Basic Pasta Dough

MAKES about 9 oz/250 g pasta

1 cup white bread flour, plus extra
    for dusting
⅔ cup fine semolina
1 tsp salt
1 tbsp olive oil
2 eggs
1–2 tbsp hot water

1 Sift the flour, semolina and salt into a large bowl and make a well in the center. Pour in the olive oil and add the eggs. Add 1 tablespoon of hot water and, using your fingertips, work to form a smooth dough. Sprinkle on a little more water if necessary to make the dough pliable.

2 Knead the dough on a lightly floured surface for 10–15 minutes or until smooth and elastic. Dust the dough with more flour if your fingers become sticky.

3 Divide the dough into 2 equal pieces. Cover a surface with a clean dish towel and dust it liberally with flour. Place 1 portion of the dough on the floured dish towel and roll it out as thinly and evenly as possible,

stretching the dough gently until the pattern of the weave shows through. Cover it with another dish towel. Roll out the second piece in the same way.

4 Use a ruler and a sharp knife to cut long, thin strips for noodles, or small confectionery cutters to cut rounds, star shapes or even an assortment of other decorative shapes. Cover the dough shapes with a clean dish towel and leave them in a cool place (not a refrigerator) for 30–45 minutes to become partly dry. To dry ribbons, place a dish towel over the back of a chair and hang the ribbons over it. Use this fresh pasta in the recipe of your choice.

Basic Pizza Dough

MAKES 1 x 10-inch/25-cm pizza

1½ cup all-purpose flour, plus extra
   for dusting
1 tsp salt
1 tsp active dry yeast
6 tbsp lukewarm water
1 tbsp olive oil

1 Sift the flour and salt into a large bowl and add the yeast. Pour in the water and olive oil and mix to a dough. Knead for 5 minutes, then let "prove" until doubled in size.

2 Punch the air out from the dough, then knead lightly. Roll it out on a lightly floured surface, ready for use.

Ragù Sauce

MAKES about 1 pint/600 ml

3 tbsp olive oil
3 tbsp butter
2 large onions, chopped
4 celery stalks, sliced thinly
1 cup chopped bacon
2 garlic cloves, chopped
4½ cups ground beef
2 tbsp tomato paste
1 tbsp flour
14 oz/400 g canned chopped tomatoes
⅔ cup beef bouillon
⅔ cup red wine
2 tsp dried oregano
½ tsp freshly grated nutmeg
salt and pepper

1 Heat the oil and butter in a large pan over medium heat. Add the onions, celery, and bacon and cook for 5 minutes, stirring.

2 Stir in the garlic and ground beef and cook, stirring, until the meat is sealed all over. Reduce the heat and let simmer for 10 minutes, stirring occasionally.

3 Increase the heat to medium, stir in the tomato paste and flour, and cook for 1–2 minutes. Add the tomatoes, bouillon, and red wine and bring to a boil, stirring. Season to taste with salt and pepper, then stir in the oregano and nutmeg. Reduce the heat, then cover and let simmer for about 45 minutes, stirring occasionally. The sauce is now ready to use.

Italian Cheese Sauce

MAKES about 10 fl oz/300 ml

2 tbsp butter
¼ cup all-purpose flour
1¼ cups hot milk
pinch of freshly grated nutmeg
pinch of dried thyme
2 tbsp white wine vinegar
3 tbsp heavy cream
½ cup freshly grated mozzarella cheese
⅔ cup freshly grated Parmesan cheese
1 tsp English mustard
2 tbsp sour cream
salt and pepper

1 Melt the butter in a pan and stir in the flour. Cook, stirring, until the roux is light crumbly. Gradually stir in the milk. Cook, stirring, for 10 minutes until thick and smooth.

2 Add the nutmeg, thyme, vinegar, and seasoning. Stir in the heavy cream, the cheeses, mustard, and sour cream and mix until blended.

Pesto Sauce

MAKES about 10 fl oz/300 ml

2 cups finely chopped fresh parsley
2 garlic cloves, minced
½ cup pine nuts, crushed
2 tbsp chopped fresh basil leaves
⅔ cup freshly grated Parmesan cheese
⅔ cup olive oil
white pepper

1 Put all the ingredients into a food processor and process for 2 minutes. Season with white pepper, transfer to a pitcher, cover, and let chill until ready to use.

How to Use This Book

Each recipe contains a wealth of useful information, including a breakdown of nutritional quantities, preparation and cooking times, and level of difficulty. All of this information is explained in detail below.

A full-color photograph of the finished dish.

BAKING

This simple combination of fudgy meringue topped with mascarpone and raspberries is the perfect finale to any meal.

Brown Sugar Pavlovas

SERVES 4
2 large egg whites
1 tsp cornflour
1 tsp raspberry vinegar
¼ cup light brown sugar, crushed free of lumps
2 tbsp red currant jelly
2 tbsp unsweetened orange juice
¼ cup lowfat mascarpone cheese
1 cup raspberries, thawed if frozen
rose-scented geranium leaves, to decorate (optional)

1 Line a large cookie sheet with baking parchment. Whisk the egg whites until very stiff and dry. Gently fold in the cornstarch and vinegar.

2 Gradually whisk in the sugar, a spoonful at a time, until the mixture is thick and glossy.

3 Divide the mixture into 4 portions and spoon onto the prepared cookie sheet, spaced well apart. Smooth each portion into a circle, 4 inches/10 cm in diameter, and bake in a preheated oven, 300°F/150°C, for 40–45 minutes until lightly browned and crisp. Remove from the oven and let cool on the cookie sheet.

4 Place the red currant jelly and orange juice in a small saucepan and heat, stirring constantly, until melted. Let cool for 10 minutes.

5 Using a spatula, carefully remove each pavlova from the baking parchment and transfer to 4 serving plates. Top with the mascarpone and the raspberries. Glaze the fruit with the red currant jelly and orange glaze, and decorate with the geranium leaves, if using.

NUTRITION
Calories 155; Sugars 34 g; Protein 5 g; Carbohydrate 35 g; Fat 0.2 g; Saturates 0 g

⊗⊗ easy
⊙ 1 hr
🕐 1 hr

🕐 COOK'S TIP
Make a large pavlova by forming the meringue into a 7-inch/18-cm circle on a lined cookie sheet. Bake in a preheated oven for 1 hour.

The ingredients for each recipe are listed in the order that they are used.

The nutritional information provided for each recipe is per serving or per portion. Optional ingredients, variations or serving suggestions have not been included in the calculations.

The method is clearly explained with step-by-step instructions that are easy to follow.

Cook's Tips provide useful information regarding ingredients or cooking techniques.

⭐ The number of stars represents the difficulty of each recipe, ranging from very easy (1 star) to challenging (4 stars).

🕐 This amount of time represents the preparation of ingredients, including cooling, chilling, and soaking times.

🕐 This represents the cooking time.

Snacks *and* Appetizers

With so many fresh ingredients readily available, it is very easy to create some deliciously different appetizers to make the perfect introduction to any meal. The ideas in this chapter are an inspiration to cook and a treat to eat, and they give an edge to the appetite that makes the main course even more enjoyable. When choosing an appetizer, make sure that you provide a good balance of flavors, colors, and textures that offer plenty of variety and contrast. Balance the nature of the recipes too—a rich main course is best preceded by a light appetizer to stimulate the taste buds.

This dish combines layers of succulent eggplant, tomato sauce, mozzarella, and Parmesan cheese to create a tasty appetizer.

Eggplant Bake

SERVES 4

3–4 tbsp olive oil
2 garlic cloves, crushed
2 large eggplants
3½ oz/100 g mozzarella cheese, sliced thinly
generous ¾ cup strained tomatoes
scant ⅔ cup freshly grated Parmesan cheese
assorted salad greens, to serve

1 Heat 2 tablespoons of the olive oil in a large skillet over low heat. Add the garlic and sauté for 30 seconds.

2 Slice the eggplants lengthwise. Add the slices to the skillet and cook in the oil for 3–4 minutes on each side or until tender. (You will probably have to cook them in batches, so add the remaining oil as necessary.)

3 Remove the eggplants with a draining spoon and drain on paper towels.

4 Place a layer of eggplant slices in a large, shallow ovenproof dish. Cover the eggplants with a layer of mozzarella cheese, then pour over one-third of the strained tomatoes. Continue layering in the same order, finishing with a layer of strained tomatoes on top.

5 Sprinkle the grated Parmesan cheese evenly over the top and bake in a preheated oven, 400°F/200°C, for about 25–30 minutes or until the top is golden-brown and bubbling.

6 Transfer the bake to 4 warmed serving plates and serve warm or cold with salad greens.

NUTRITION
Calories *232*; Sugars *8 g*; Protein *10 g*;
Carbohydrate *8 g*; Fat *18 g*; Saturates *6 g*

moderate

5 mins

45 mins

This is an impressive dinner-party dish—serve it as an appetizer. You will find large tomatoes are easier to fill.

Stuffed Tomatoes

1 Rinse the tomatoes, cut off the tops, and scoop out the flesh. Grease an ovenproof dish with the butter and place the tomatoes in the dish.

2 Heat the vegetable oil in a heavy-based pan over medium heat. Add the onion and cook, stirring frequently, until golden.

3 Reduce the heat and add the ginger, garlic, pepper, salt, and garam masala. Cook the mixture, stirring occasionally, for 3–5 minutes.

4 Add the ground lamb to the pan and cook, stirring frequently, for about 10–15 minutes or until it has lost its pink color.

5 Add the chile and cilantro leaves and continue cooking for 3–5 minutes.

6 Spoon the lamb mixture into the tomatoes and replace the tops. Bake the tomatoes in a preheated oven, 350°F/180°C, for 15–20 minutes.

7 Transfer the tomatoes to 4 serving plates, garnish with lemon wedges, and serve hot with salad greens.

SERVES 4

6 large, firm tomatoes
4 tbsp unsalted butter
5 tbsp vegetable oil
1 onion, chopped finely
1 tsp finely chopped fresh gingerroot
1 tsp crushed fresh garlic
1 tsp pepper
1 tsp salt
½ tsp garam masala
4 cups ground lamb
1 fresh green chile
handful of fresh cilantro leaves
lemon wedges, to garnish
salad greens, to serve

NUTRITION
Calories *290*; Sugars *5 g*; Protein *17 g*;
Carbohydrate *8 g*; Fat *23 g*; Saturates *9 g*

⭐⭐⭐   moderate
🕐   5 mins
🕐   45 mins

🧑‍🍳 **COOK'S TIP**

You could use the same recipe to fill red or green bell peppers, if you prefer.

Ready-made individual pizza doughs are covered with a chile-tomato sauce and topped with kidney beans, cheese, and jalapeño chiles.

Mexican-Style Pizzas

SERVES 4

4 ready-made, precooked individual
   pizza doughs
1 tbsp olive oil
7 oz/200 g canned chopped tomatoes with
   garlic and herbs
2 tbsp tomato paste
7 oz/200 g canned kidney beans, drained
   and rinsed
²/₃ cup corn kernels, thawed if frozen
1–2 tsp chili sauce
1 large red onion, shredded
1 cup grated reduced-fat sharp cheese
1 large green chile, seeded and sliced
   into rings
salt and pepper

1 Place the pizza doughs on a cookie sheet and brush them with the olive oil.

2 Mix the chopped tomatoes, tomato paste, kidney beans, and corn together in a large bowl and add chile sauce to taste. Season with salt and pepper.

3 Using a spoon, spread the tomato and kidney bean mixture evenly over each pizza dough to cover.

4 Top each pizza with shredded onion and sprinkle with some grated sharp cheese and a few slices of chile to taste.

5 Bake the pizza in a preheated oven, 425°F/220°C, for about 20 minutes or until the vegetables are tender, the cheese has melted, and the dough is crisp and golden.

6 Remove the pizzas from the cookie sheet and transfer to 4 warmed serving plates. Serve immediately.

NUTRITION

Calories *350*; Sugars *8 g*; Protein *18 g*;
Carbohydrate *49 g*; Fat *10 g*; Saturates *3 g*

easy

10 mins

20 mins

🍳 **COOK'S TIP**

Serve a Mexican-style salad with this pizza. Arrange sliced tomatoes, fresh cilantro leaves, and a few slices of a small, ripe avocado on a serving plate. Sprinkle with fresh lime juice and coarse sea salt.

These crisp pies are filled with a tasty onion, garlic, and parsley mixture, making them ideal for school and office snacks.

Cheese *and* Onion Pies

1 Heat the vegetable oil in a skillet over low heat. Add the onions and garlic and cook for 10–15 minutes or until the onions are softened. Remove the skillet from the heat, stir in the parsley and cheese, and season to taste with salt and pepper.

2 To make the pie dough, sift the flour and salt into a large bowl. Add the butter and rub it in with your fingertips until the mixture resembles bread crumbs. Gradually stir in the water and mix to form a dough.

3 Roll out the dough on a lightly floured surface and divide it into 8 portions. Roll out each portion into a circle 4 inches/10 cm across and use half of the circles to line 4 individual tart pans.

4 Fill each circle with one-quarter of the cheese and onion mixture. Cover with the remaining 4 pie dough circles. Make a slit in the top of each pie with the point of a knife to allow steam to escape during cooking and seal the edges with the back of a teaspoon.

5 Bake in a preheated oven, 425°F/220°C, for 20 minutes. Transfer the pies to 4 large serving plates, if serving hot, or to a wire rack, if serving cold.

SERVES 4

3 tbsp vegetable oil
4 onions, sliced thinly
4 garlic cloves, crushed
4 tbsp finely chopped fresh parsley
¾ cup grated sharp cheese
salt and pepper

pie dough
1¼ cups all-purpose flour, plus extra for dusting
½ tsp salt
⅓ cup butter, cut into small pieces
3–4 tbsp water

NUTRITION
Calories *544*; Sugars *9 g*; Protein *11 g*; Carbohydrate *47 g*; Fat *36 g*; Saturates *18 g*

⭐⭐ easy

🕐 15 mins

🕐 35 mins

🍳 **COOK'S TIP**

You can prepare the onion filling in advance and store it in the refrigerator until required.

A crisp lining of bread is filled with garlic butter and pine nuts to make a delightful and unusual appetizer or snack.

Garlic *and* Pine Nut Tarts

SERVES 4

4 slices whole-wheat or Granary bread
½ cup pine nuts
¾ cup butter
5 garlic cloves, halved
2 tbsp chopped fresh oregano
4 pitted black olives, halved
fresh oregano sprigs, to garnish

1 Using a rolling pin, flatten the bread slightly. Using a cookie cutter, cut out 4 circles of bread to fit your individual tart pans—they should measure about 4 inches/10 cm across. Set aside the offcuts of bread and leave them in the refrigerator for 10 minutes or until required.

2 Meanwhile, place the pine nuts on a small cookie sheet and toast under a preheated hot broiler for 2–3 minutes or until golden.

3 Put the bread offcuts, pine nuts, butter, garlic, and oregano into a food processor and process for 20 seconds. Alternatively, pound the ingredients by hand in a mortar with a pestle. The mixture should have a coarse texture.

4 Spoon the pine nut and butter mixture into the lined pans and top with the olive halves. Bake in a preheated oven, 400°F/200°C, for 10–15 minutes or until golden.

5 Transfer the tarts to 4 warmed serving plates and garnish with a few sprigs of fresh oregano. Serve warm.

NUTRITION
Calories *435*; Sugars *1 g*; Protein *6 g*;
Carbohydrate *17 g*; Fat *39 g*; Saturates *20 g*

★★★   moderate

🕐   20 mins

🕐   20 mins

👨‍🍳 COOK'S TIP

Chill 7 oz/200 g puff pie dough for 20 minutes, then use to line 4 tart pans. Cover with foil, and bake for 10 minutes. Remove the foil and bake for 3–4 minutes. Cool. Continue from step 2, adding 2 tablespoons of bread crumbs to the mixture.

This is an unusual dish from India, in that the eggplants are first baked in the oven, then cooked in a pan.

Eggplants *and* Yogurt

1 Rinse the eggplants and pat dry with paper towels.

2 Place the eggplants in an ovenproof dish and bake in a preheated oven, 325°F/160°C, for 45 minutes. Remove from the oven and let cool.

3 Using a spoon, scoop out the eggplant flesh and set aside.

4 Heat the vegetable oil in a heavy-based pan over low heat. Add the onions and cumin seeds and cook, stirring occasionally, for 1–2 minutes.

5 Add the chile powder, salt, yogurt, and mint sauce to the pan, and stir thoroughly to mix. Reduce the heat.

6 Add the eggplant flesh to the onion and yogurt mixture and cook over low heat for 5–7 minutes or until all of the liquid has been absorbed and the mixture has become quite dry.

7 Transfer the eggplant and yogurt mixture to a serving dish and garnish with shredded mint. Serve immediately with freshly cooked rice.

SERVES 4

2 medium eggplants
4 tbsp vegetable oil
1 onion, sliced
1 tsp white cumin seeds
1 tsp chile powder
1 tsp salt
3 tbsp plain yogurt
½ tsp mint sauce
shredded fresh mint leaves, to garnish
freshly cooked rice, to serve

NUTRITION
Calories *147*; Sugars *6 g*; Protein *3 g*; Carbohydrate *8 g*; Fat *11 g*; Saturates *1 g*

⊗⊗ easy
⊘ 5 mins
◕ 1 hr 5 mins

🍳 COOK'S TIP

Rich in protein and calcium, yogurt plays a very important part in Indian cooking. Thick unsweetened yogurt most closely resembles the yogurt made in many Indian homes.

This is a classic combination in which the smooth, creamy cheese balances the sharper taste of the spinach.

Spinach *and* Ricotta Shells

SERVES 4

14 oz/400 g dried lumache rigate grande pasta
5 tbsp olive oil
1 cup fresh white bread crumbs
½ cup milk
10½ oz/300 g frozen spinach, thawed and drained
1 cup ricotta cheese
pinch of freshly grated nutmeg
14 oz/400 g canned chopped tomatoes, drained
1 garlic clove, crushed
salt and pepper

1 Bring a large pan of lightly salted water to a boil over medium heat. Add the lumache and 1 tablespoon of the olive oil, bring back to a boil, and cook for 8–10 minutes until tender but still firm to the bite. Drain the pasta, refresh under cold water, drain again, and set aside until required.

2 Put the bread crumbs, milk, and 3 tablespoons of the remaining olive oil in a food processor and process to combine.

3 Add the spinach and ricotta cheese to the food processor and process to a smooth mixture. Transfer to a bowl, stir in the nutmeg, and season to taste with salt and pepper.

4 Mix the tomatoes, garlic, and the remaining olive oil together, then spoon the mixture into the bottom of a large ovenproof dish.

5 Using a teaspoon, fill the lumache with the spinach and ricotta mixture and arrange them on top of the tomato mixture in the dish. Cover with foil and bake in a preheated oven, 350°F/180°C, for 20 minutes. Serve hot.

NUTRITION
Calories *672*; Sugars *10 g*; Protein *23 g*; Carbohydrate *93 g*; Fat *26 g*; Saturates *8 g*

moderate

10 mins

40 mins

COOK'S TIP

Ricotta is a creamy Italian cheese traditionally made from sheeps' milk whey. It is soft and white, with a smooth texture and a slightly sweet flavor. It should be used within 2–3 days of purchase.

This is a traditional Italian recipe but, if you prefer a less rich version, you can simply omit the eggs.

Gnocchi Romana

1 Pour the milk into a pan and bring to a boil over low heat. Remove the pan from the heat and stir in the nutmeg and 2 tablespoons of the butter. Season to taste with salt and pepper.

2 Gradually stir the semolina into the milk, whisking to prevent lumps forming, and return the pan to low heat. Let simmer, stirring constantly, for 10 minutes or until very thick.

3 Beat ²/₄ cup of the Parmesan cheese into the semolina mixture, then beat in the eggs. Continue beating until smooth, then let cool slightly.

4 Spread out the semolina mixture in a layer on a sheet of baking parchment, smoothing the surface with a damp spatula—it should be ½ inch/1 cm thick. Let cool completely, then chill in the refrigerator for 1 hour.

5 Once chilled, cut out circles of gnocchi, measuring about 1½ inches/4 cm in diameter, using a plain, greased dough cutter.

6 Grease a shallow ovenproof dish or 4 individual ovenproof dishes. Lay the gnocchi trimmings in the bottom of the dish or dishes and arrange the circles of gnocchi on top, slightly overlapping each other.

7 Melt the remaining butter and drizzle it over the gnocchi. Sprinkle over the remaining Parmesan cheese, then sprinkle over the Swiss cheese.

8 Bake in a preheated oven, 400°F/200°C, for 25–30 minutes or until crisp and golden-brown. Garnish with fresh basil and serve with salad greens.

SERVES 4

scant 4 cups milk
pinch of freshly grated nutmeg
6 tbsp butter, plus extra for greasing
1¼ cups semolina
generous 1 cup freshly grated
    Parmesan cheese
2 eggs, beaten
½ cup grated Swiss cheese
salt and pepper
fresh basil sprigs, to garnish
salad greens, to serve

NUTRITION
Calories 709; Sugars 9 g; Protein 32 g;
Carbohydrate 58 g; Fat 41 g; Saturates 25 g

⭐⭐⭐   moderate
            1 hr 15 mins
            45 mins

Serve this dish while the cheese is still hot and melted, as cooked cheese turns very rubbery if it is allowed to cool down.

Three Cheese Bake

SERVES 4

1 tbsp butter, for greasing
14 oz/400 g dried penne
1 tbsp olive oil
2 eggs, beaten
1½ cups ricotta cheese
4 sprigs fresh basil
1 cup grated mozzarella or halloumi cheese
⅔ cup freshly grated Parmesan cheese
salt and pepper
fresh basil leaves, to garnish (optional)

1 Lightly grease a large ovenproof dish with the butter.

2 Bring a large pan of lightly salted water to a boil over medium heat. Add the penne and olive oil, bring back to a boil, and cook for 8–10 minutes or until tender but still firm to the bite. Drain the pasta and keep warm.

3 Beat the eggs into the ricotta cheese. Season to taste with salt and pepper.

4 Spoon half of the penne into the bottom of the prepared dish and cover with half of the basil leaves.

5 Spoon over half of the ricotta cheese mixture. Sprinkle over the mozzarella or halloumi cheese and top with the remaining basil leaves. Cover with the remaining penne, then spoon over the remaining ricotta cheese mixture. Lightly sprinkle the Parmesan cheese over the top.

6 Bake in a preheated oven, 375°F/190°C, for 30–40 minutes or until golden-brown and the topping is hot and bubbling. Garnish with fresh basil leaves, if desired, and serve hot straight from the dish.

NUTRITION
Calories *710*; Sugars *6 g*; Protein *34 g*;
Carbohydrate *80 g*; Fat *30 g*; Saturates *16 g*

moderate

5 mins

1 hr

🍴 **COOK'S TIP**

Try substituting smoked Bavarian cheese for the mozzarella or halloumi and grated sharp cheese for the Parmesan cheese, for a slightly different, but just as delicious flavor.

These large pasta nests look impressive when presented filled with broiled mixed vegetables and they taste delicious.

Vegetable Pasta Nests

1 Bring a large pan of lightly salted water to a boil over medium heat. Add the spaghetti, bring back to a boil, and cook for 8–10 minutes or until tender, but still firm to the bite. Drain the spaghetti in a strainer and set aside.

2 Place the eggplant, zucchini, and bell pepper on a large cookie sheet.

3 Mix the oil and garlic together in a bowl and pour over the vegetables, tossing to coat all over.

4 Cook the vegetables under a preheated hot broiler for 10 minutes, turning, until tender and lightly charred. Set aside and keep warm.

5 Grease 4 large, shallow muffin pans with a little butter and divide the spaghetti among them. Using 2 forks, curl the spaghetti to form nests.

6 Brush the pasta nests with the melted butter and sprinkle with the bread crumbs. Bake in a preheated oven, 400°F/200°C, for 15 minutes or until golden. Remove the pasta nests from the pans and transfer to 4 serving plates. Divide the broiled vegetables among the pasta nests and season to taste with salt and pepper. Garnish with fresh parsley and serve hot.

SERVES 4

6 oz/175 g dried spaghetti
1 eggplant, halved and sliced
1 zucchini, diced
1 red bell pepper, seeded and diagonally chopped
6 tbsp olive oil
2 garlic cloves, crushed
4 tbsp butter, melted, plus extra for greasing
1 tbsp dry white bread crumbs
salt and pepper
fresh Italian parsley sprigs, to garnish

NUTRITION
Calories *392*; Sugars *1 g*; Protein *6 g*;
Carbohydrate *32 g*; Fat *28 g*; Saturates *9 g*

⭐⭐⭐ moderate

🕐 25 mins

🕐 40 mins

👨‍🍳 COOK'S TIP

The Italian term, *al dente* means "to the bite" and describes cooked pasta that is not too soft, but still has a "bite" to it.

This warming and
satisfying dish would
make a tasty snack or even
a light family meal on a
dreary winter's evening.

Macaroni Bake

SERVES 4

4 cups dried short-cut macaroni
1 tbsp olive oil
4 tbsp beef drippings or olive oil
1 lb/450 g potatoes, peeled and thinly sliced
1 lb/450 g onions, sliced
2 cups grated mozzarella cheese
²/₃ cup heavy cream
salt and pepper
cracked black pepper, to garnish
crusty brown bread and butter, to serve

1 Bring a large pan of lightly salted water to a boil over medium heat. Add the macaroni and 1 tbsp of olive oil, bring back to a boil, and cook for 12 minutes or until tender but still firm to the bite. Drain thoroughly and set aside.

2 Heat the drippings or olive oil in a large ovenproof casserole over low heat, then remove the casserole from the heat.

3 Make alternate layers of potatoes, onions, macaroni, and grated mozzarella in the casserole, seasoning well with salt and pepper between each layer and finishing with a layer of cheese on top. Finally, pour the cream over the top layer of cheese.

4 Bake in a preheated oven, 400°F/200°C, for 25 minutes. Remove the dish from the oven and carefully brown the top of the bake under a preheated hot broiler.

5 Garnish the bake with cracked pepper and serve straight from the dish with crusty brown bread and butter as a main course. Alternatively, serve as a vegetable accompaniment with your favorite main course.

NUTRITION

Calories 728; Sugars 11 g; Protein 17 g;
Carbohydrate 75 g; Fat 42 g; Saturates 23 g

moderate

15 mins

45 mins

COOK'S TIP

For a stronger flavor, use *mozzarella affumicata*, a smoked version of this cheese, or Swiss cheese, instead of the normal mozzarella cheese.

This makes an excellent light meal when served with a topping of pesto or anchovy sauce and crisp salad greens.

Pancetta *and* Romano Cakes

1 Grease a cookie sheet with butter. Cook the pancetta under a preheated hot broiler until cooked. Let the pancetta cool, then chop finely.

2 Sift the flour and a pinch of salt into a large bowl. Add the butter and rub in with your fingertips until the mixture resembles bread crumbs. Add the pancetta and ¼ cup of the grated cheese.

3 Mix the milk, tomato ketchup, and Worcestershire sauce together and add to the dry ingredients, mixing well to form a soft dough.

4 Roll out the dough on a lightly floured surface to make a 7-inch/18-cm circle. Brush with a little milk to glaze and cut into 8 wedges.

5 Arrange the dough wedges on the prepared cookie sheet and sprinkle over the remaining grated cheese. Bake in a preheated oven, 400°F/200°C, for about 20 minutes.

6 Meanwhile, bring a large pan of lightly salted water to a boil over medium heat. Add the farfalle and the olive oil, bring back to a boil, and cook for about 8–10 minutes or until just tender but still firm to the bite. Drain and transfer to a large serving dish. Top with the pancetta and romano cakes. Serve with the sauce of your choice and salad greens.

SERVES 4

2 tbsp butter, plus extra for greasing
3½ oz/100 g pancetta, rind removed
2 cups self-rising flour, plus extra for dusting
¾ cup grated romano cheese
⅔ cup milk, plus extra for glazing
1 tbsp tomato ketchup
1 tsp Worcestershire sauce
14 oz/400 g dried farfalle
1 tbsp olive oil
salt

to serve

3 tbsp Pesto Sauce (see page 15) or anchovy sauce (optional)
salad greens, to serve

NUTRITION
Calories *619*; Sugars *4 g*; Protein *22 g*; Carbohydrate *71 g*; Fat *29 g*; Saturates *8 g*

✪✪✪✪ challenging
🕐 20 mins
🕐 40 mins

These tomato-flavored tarts should be eaten as fresh as possible to enjoy the flaky and crisp buttery puff pastry.

Fresh Tomato Tarts

SERVES 6

9 oz/250 g ready-made puff pie dough, thawed if frozen
all-purpose flour, for dusting
1 egg, beaten
2 tbsp Pesto Sauce (see page 15)
6 plum tomatoes, sliced
salt and pepper
fresh thyme leaves, to garnish (optional)

1 Roll out the pie dough on a lightly floured surface to a rectangle measuring 12 x 10 inches/30 x 25 cm.

2 Cut the rectangle in half and divide each half into 3 pieces to make 6 even-size rectangles. Let chill in the refrigerator for 20 minutes.

3 Lightly score the edges of the pie dough rectangles and brush them with the beaten egg.

4 Spread the pesto over the rectangles, dividing it equally among them, leaving a 1-inch/2.5-cm border around each one.

5 Arrange the tomato slices along the center of each rectangle on top of the pesto. Season well with salt and pepper and lightly sprinkle with fresh thyme leaves, if using.

6 Bake in a preheated oven, 400°F/200°C, for 15–20 minutes or until well risen and golden-brown.

7 Transfer the tomato tarts to 6 warmed serving plates and serve while they are still piping hot.

NUTRITION
Calories 217; Sugars 3 g; Protein 5 g;
Carbohydrate 18 g; Fat 14 g; Saturates 1 g

⭐⭐⭐ moderate
🕑 35 mins
🕐 20 mins

🍽 **COOK'S TIP**

Instead of individual tarts, roll the dough out to form 1 large rectangle. Spoon over the pesto and arrange the tomatoes over the top.

This tart is full of color and flavor from the zucchini and red and green bell peppers. It makes a great change from a quiche Lorraine.

Provençal Tart

1 Roll out the pie dough on a lightly floured surface and use to line an 8-inch/20-cm loose-bottom tart pan. Let chill in the refrigerator for 20 minutes.

2 Meanwhile, heat 2 tablespoons of the olive oil in a skillet over low heat. Add the red and green bell peppers and cook, stirring frequently, for 8 minutes or until softened.

3 Whisk the cream and egg together in a bowl and season to taste with salt and pepper. Stir in the cooked bell peppers.

4 Heat the remaining olive oil in a skillet over medium heat. Add the zucchini slices and cook for 4–5 minutes until lightly browned.

5 Pour the egg and bell pepper mixture into the tart shell.

6 Arrange the zucchini slices around the edge of the tart.

7 Bake in a preheated oven, 350°F/180°C, for 35–40 minutes or until just set and golden-brown. Serve immediately or let cool and serve cold.

SERVES 6

9 oz/250 g ready-made puff pie dough, thawed if frozen
all-purpose flour, for dusting
3 tbsp olive oil
2 red bell peppers, seeded and diced
2 green bell peppers, seeded and diced
²⁄₃ cup heavy cream
1 egg
2 zucchini, sliced
salt and pepper

NUTRITION
Calories 355; Sugars 5 g; Protein 5 g; Carbohydrate 21 g; Fat 29 g; Saturates 9 g

⭐⭐   easy

🤏   10 mins

🕐   55 mins

🍳 **COOK'S TIP**

This recipe could be used to make 6 individual tarts—use 6 x 4-inch/15 x 10-cm pans and bake them for 20 minutes.

This is a French variation of the classic Italian pizza but is made with ready-made puff pie dough. It is perfect for outdoor eating.

Pissaladière

SERVES 8

1 tbsp butter, for greasing
4 tbsp olive oil
1 lb 9 oz/700 g red onions, sliced thinly
2 garlic cloves, crushed
2 tsp superfine sugar
2 tbsp red wine vinegar
12 oz/350 g ready-made puff pie dough, thawed if frozen
all-purpose flour, for dusting
salt and pepper

topping
3½ oz/100 g canned anchovy fillets
12 green pitted olives
1 tsp dried marjoram

NUTRITION
Calories *290*; Sugars *7 g*; Protein *7 g*;
Carbohydrate *25 g*; Fat *19 g*; Saturates *1 g*

✪✪✪   moderate

🖐   10 mins

🕐   55 mins

1 Lightly grease an edged cookie sheet with the butter. Heat the olive oil in a large pan over low heat. Add the onions and garlic and cook for 30 minutes, stirring occasionally.

2 Add the sugar and red wine vinegar to the pan and season with plenty of salt and pepper.

3 Roll out the pie dough on a lightly floured surface to a rectangle measuring about 13 x 9 inches/33 x 23 cm. Carefully transfer the dough rectangle to the prepared cookie sheet, pushing the dough well into the corners.

4 Spread the onion mixture evenly over the dough.

5 Drain and arrange the anchovy fillets in a criss-cross pattern on top, dot with the green olives, then sprinkle with the dried marjoram.

6 Bake in a preheated oven, 425°F/220°C, for about 20–25 minutes until the pissaladière is lightly golden. Serve piping hot, straight from the oven.

🍳 **COOK'S TIP**

Cut the baked pissaladière into squares or triangles for easy finger food at a party or barbecue grill.

These lattice pies are equally delicious served hot or cold. They make a good picnic food served with salad greens.

Ham *and* Cheese Lattice Pies

1 Lightly grease 2 cookie sheets with the butter.

2 Roll out the pie dough on a lightly floured surface and cut out 12 rectangles measuring 6 x 2 inches/15 x 5 cm. Place the rectangles on the prepared cookie sheets and let chill in the refrigerator for 30 minutes.

3 Meanwhile, mix the ham, soft cheese, and chives in a small bowl. Season to taste with pepper, then spread the mixture along the center of 6 of the rectangles, leaving a 1-inch/2.5-cm border around each one. Brush the border with the beaten egg.

4 To make the lattice pattern, fold the remaining rectangles lengthwise, then, leaving a 1-inch/2.5-cm border, cut vertical lines across the folded edge.

5 Unfold the latticed rectangles and place them over the rectangles topped with the ham and cheese mixture. Seal the dough edges well and lightly sprinkle with the Parmesan cheese. Bake in a preheated oven, 350°F/180°C, for 15–20 minutes. Serve hot or cold.

SERVES   6

2 tbsp butter, for greasing
9 oz/250 g ready-made puff pie dough
all-purpose flour, for dusting
generous ⅓ cup finely chopped ham
4½ oz/125 g full fat soft cheese
2 tbsp chopped fresh chives
1 egg, beaten
scant ½ cup freshly grated Parmesan cheese
pepper

NUTRITION
Calories *257*; Sugars *1 g*; Protein *8 g*;
Carbohydrate *16 g*; Fat *19 g*; Saturates *5 g*

★★★   moderate

🕐   45 mins

🕐   20 mins

COOK'S TIP

These pies can be made in advance then frozen uncooked and baked fresh when required.

Savory Meals

This chapter presents a mouthwatering array of savory dishes to tempt any palate, including pies, pastries, tarts, and flans, as well as a variety of delicious savory bakes. The choice is huge, including Cheese Dessert, Red Onion Tart Tatin, and Asparagus and Cheese Tart. Fish fans can choose from a wide menu, including Smoky Fish Pie, Seafood Lasagna, and Fillets of Snapper and Pasta. Meat and poultry dishes include Prosciutto-Wrapped Chicken, Rich Beef Stew, and Italian Chicken Parcels.

This savory cheese pudding is very like a soufflé in texture, but it does not rise like a traditional soufflé.

Cheese Pudding

SERVES 4

1 tbsp butter, for greasing
2½ cups fresh white bread crumbs
1 cup grated Swiss cheese
⅔ cup lukewarm milk
½ cup butter, melted
2 eggs, separated
salt and pepper
2 tbsp chopped fresh parsley

1 Grease a 4-cup/1-liter ovenproof dish with a little butter.

2 Mix the bread crumbs and cheese together in a bowl. Pour over the milk and stir to mix. Add the melted butter, egg yolks, parsley, and salt and pepper to taste. Mix well.

3 Whisk the egg whites in a clean bowl until they form soft peaks. Gently fold the cheese mixture into the egg whites, using a figure-eight movement.

4 Transfer the mixture to the prepared ovenproof dish and gently smooth the surface with a knife.

5 Bake in a preheated oven, 375°F/190°C, for about 45 minutes or until golden and slightly risen, and a toothpick inserted into the center of the pudding comes out clean. Serve hot.

NUTRITION
Calories 483; Sugars 3 g; Protein 15 g;
Carbohydrate 20 g; Fat 39 g; Saturates 24 g

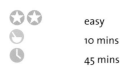

easy

10 mins

45 mins

🍴 **COOK'S TIP**

For a slightly healthier alternative, make the cheese pudding with fresh whole-wheat bread crumbs instead of the white bread crumbs.

Ready-made puff pie dough works well in this recipe and means you can create a tasty savory tart in very little time.

Red Onion Tart Tatin

1 Place the butter and sugar in a 9-inch/23-cm ovenproof skillet and cook over medium heat until the butter has melted and the sugar has dissolved.

2 Add the red onion fourths and let sweat over low heat, stirring occasionally, for 10–15 minutes or until golden.

3 Add the vinegar and thyme leaves to the skillet. Season to taste with salt and pepper, then let simmer over medium heat until the liquid has reduced and the red onion pieces are coated in the buttery sauce.

4 Roll out the pie dough on a lightly floured surface into a circle slightly larger than the skillet. Place the pie dough over the onion mixture in the skillet and gently press down, carefully tucking in the edges to seal the dough.

5 Bake in a preheated oven, 350°F/180°C, for 20–25 minutes until golden-brown. Remove the skillet from the oven and let stand for 10 minutes.

6 To turn out, place a serving plate over the skillet and, holding them together, carefully invert them both so that the pie dough becomes the bottom of the tart. Serve warm.

SERVES 4

4 tbsp butter
2 tbsp sugar
1 lb 2 oz/500 g red onions, cut into fourths
3 tbsp red wine vinegar
2 tbsp fresh thyme leaves
9 oz/250 g ready-made puff pie dough, thawed if frozen
all-purpose flour, for dusting
salt and pepper

COOK'S TIP

Replace the red onions with shallots, leaving them whole, if you prefer.

NUTRITION
Calories 398; Sugars 14 g; Protein 5 g; Carbohydrate 40 g; Fat 25 g; Saturates 7 g

⊗⊗⊗ moderate
🕐 15 mins
🕐 50 mins

Fresh asparagus is now readily available all year round, so you can make this tasty and attractive dish at any time.

Asparagus *and* Cheese Tart

SERVES 6

9 oz/250 g ready-made unsweetened pie dough, thawed if frozen
all-purpose flour, for dusting
9 oz/250 g asparagus
1 tbsp vegetable oil
1 red onion, chopped finely
2 tbsp chopped hazelnuts
7 oz/200 g goat cheese
2 eggs, beaten
4 tbsp light cream
salt and pepper

NUTRITION
Calories *360*; Sugars *4 g*; Protein *11 g*;
Carbohydrate *23 g*; Fat *25 g*; Saturates *10 g*

easy

5–10 mins

50 mins

1 Roll out the pie dough on a lightly floured surface and use to line a 9½-inch/24-cm loose-bottom tart pan. Prick the bottom of the tart shell with a fork and let chill in the refrigerator for 30 minutes.

2 Line the tart shell with foil and baking beans and bake in a preheated oven, 375°F/190°C, for about 15 minutes.

3 Remove the foil and baking beans and cook for another 15 minutes.

4 Cook the asparagus in boiling water for 2–3 minutes, drain, and cut into bite-size pieces.

5 Heat the vegetable oil in a small skillet over low heat. Add the onion and cook, stirring occasionally for about 5 minutes until softened and golden. Spoon the asparagus, onion, and hazelnuts into the prepared tart shell.

6 Beat the cheese, eggs, and cream together until smooth. Alternatively, process in a blender. Season well with salt and pepper, then pour the mixture over the asparagus, onion, and hazelnuts.

7 Bake in the preheated oven for 15–20 minutes or until the cheese filling is just set. Serve warm or cold.

🍳 **COOK'S TIP**

Omit the hazelnuts and sprinkle freshly grated Parmesan cheese over the top of the tart just before cooking in the oven, if you prefer.

This crisp tart shell is filled with succulent, caramelized onions and cheese, then baked until it melts in the mouth.

Onion Tart

1 Roll out the pie dough on a lightly floured surface and use to line a 9½-inch/24-cm loose-bottom tart pan.

2 Prick the base of the tart shell with a fork and let chill in the refrigerator for 30 minutes.

3 Meanwhile, heat the butter in a pan over low heat. Add the bacon and onions and let sweat for about 25 minutes until tender. If the onion slices start to brown, add 1 tablespoon of water to the pan.

4 Add the beaten eggs to the onion mixture and stir in the grated cheese and sage. Season to taste with salt and pepper.

5 Spoon the bacon and onion mixture into the prepared tart shell.

6 Bake in a preheated oven, 350°F/180°C, for 20–30 minutes or until the filling has just set and the pastry is golden-brown.

7 Let the tart cool slightly in the pan, then remove from the pan and serve warm or cold.

SERVES 4

9 oz/250 g ready-made unsweetened pie dough, thawed if frozen
all-purpose flour, for dusting
3 tbsp butter
generous ⅓ cup chopped bacon
1 lb 9 oz/700 g onions, sliced thinly
2 eggs, beaten
scant ⅔ cup freshly grated Parmesan cheese
1 tsp dried sage
salt and pepper

NUTRITION
Calories *394*; Sugars *7 g*; Protein *27 g*; Carbohydrate *29 g*; Fat *27 g*; Saturates *12 g*

⭐⭐   easy
🕑   5 mins
🕐   55 mins

🧑‍🍳 COOK'S TIP

For a vegetarian version of this tart, replace the bacon with the same amount of chopped mushrooms.

Pizza means "pie" in Italian. The fresh bread dough is not difficult to make but it does take a little time.

Pizza Margherita

SERVES 4

pizza dough

½ oz/15 g fresh yeast
½ tsp sugar
6 tbsp lukewarm water
1½ cups all-purpose flour, plus extra
    for dusting
1 tsp salt
1 tbsp olive oil, plus extra for oiling

topping

14 oz/400 g canned tomatoes, chopped
2 garlic cloves, crushed
2 tsp dried basil
1 tbsp olive oil
2 tbsp tomato paste
3½ oz/100 g mozzarella cheese, chopped
scant ½ cup freshly grated Parmesan cheese
salt and pepper

NUTRITION

Calories *456*; Sugars *7 g*; Protein *16 g*;
Carbohydrate *74 g*; Fat *13 g*; Saturates *5 g*

moderate

1 hr

45 mins

1 To make the pizza dough, mix the yeast, sugar, and 4 tablespoons of the water together. Let stand in a warm place for 15 minutes until frothy.

2 Mix the flour and salt together in a separate bowl and make a well in the center. Add the olive oil, the yeast mixture, and remaining water. Mix to form a smooth dough.

3 Knead the dough on a floured surface for 4–5 minutes or until smooth.

4 Return the dough to the bowl, cover with an oiled sheet of plastic wrap, and let rise for 30 minutes or until doubled in size.

5 Knead the dough for 2 minutes. Stretch it with your hands, then place it on an oiled cookie sheet, pushing out the edges until even. The dough should be no more than ¼ inch/5 mm thick because it will rise during cooking.

6 To make the topping, place the tomatoes, garlic, dried basil, and olive oil in a large skillet. Season to taste with salt and pepper and let simmer over low heat for about 20 minutes or until the sauce has thickened. Stir in the tomato paste, remove from the heat, and let cool slightly.

7 Spread the topping evenly over the pizza dough almost to the edge and top with the mozzarella and Parmesan cheeses. Bake in a preheated oven, 400°F/200°C, for 20–25 minutes or until the topping is golden-brown and bubbling. Serve hot.

This is a traditional dish from the Calabrian Mountains in southern Italy, where it is made with sun-dried tomatoes and ricotta cheese.

Tomato *and* Ricotta Pizza

1 Knead the pizza dough on a lightly floured surface for 2 minutes or until smooth and elastic.

2 Using a rolling pin, roll out the dough to form a circle, then carefully transfer it to an oiled cookie sheet, pushing out the edges until even. The dough should be no more than about ¼ inch/5 mm thick because it will rise during cooking.

3 Spread the sun-dried tomato paste evenly over the dough, then add spoonfuls of ricotta cheese, dotting them over the pizza.

4 Cut the sun-dried tomatoes into thin strips and arrange these over the top of the pizza.

5 Sprinkle the thyme leaves over the top of the pizza and season to taste with salt and pepper. Bake in a preheated oven, 400°F/200°C, for 30 minutes or the crust is golden. Serve hot.

SERVES 4

1 quantity Basic Pizza Dough (see page 15)
all-purpose flour, for dusting
1 tbsp olive oil, for oiling

topping
4 tbsp sun-dried tomato paste
⅔ cup ricotta cheese
10 sun-dried tomatoes in oil, drained
1 tbsp fresh thyme leaves
salt and pepper

NUTRITION
Calories *274*; Sugars *4 g*; Protein *8 g*;
Carbohydrate *38 g*; Fat *11 g*; Saturates *4 g*

⊛⊛⊛   moderate
◔   1 hr 15 mins
◔   30 mins

🍳 **COOK'S TIP**

Sun-dried tomatoes are also available in packages. Before using, soak them in a bowl of hot water until softened. You can use the tomato-flavored water for bouillons and soups.

This pizza is a favorite of the Romans. It is slightly unusual because the topping is made without a tomato sauce base.

Onion, Ham, *and* Cheese Pizza

SERVES 4

1 quantity Basic Pizza Dough (see page 15)
all-purpose flour. for dusting
1 tbsp olive oil, for oiling

topping
2 tbsp olive oil
9 oz/250 g onions, sliced into rings
2 garlic cloves, crushed
1 red bell pepper, seeded and diced
3½ oz/100 g prosciutto, cut into strips
3½ oz/100 g mozzarella cheese, sliced
2 tbsp fresh rosemary sprigs, stalks removed
   and coarsely chopped

1 Knead the pizza dough on a lightly floured surface for 2 minutes or until smooth and elastic.

2 Using a rolling pin, roll out the dough to form a square shape, then transfer it to an oiled cookie sheet, pushing out the edges until even. The dough should be no more than ¼-inch/5-mm thick because it will rise during cooking.

3 To make the topping, heat the olive oil in a pan over low heat. Add the onions and garlic and cook for 3 minutes. Add the bell pepper and cook for 2 minutes.

4 Cover the pan and cook the vegetables for 10 minutes, stirring occasionally, until the onions are slightly caramelized. Remove the pan from the heat and let cool slightly.

5 Spread the topping evenly over the pizza dough almost to the edge. Arrange the strips of prosciutto, mozzarella slices, and rosemary over the top.

6 Bake in a preheated oven, 400°F/200°C, for 20–25 minutes. Serve hot.

NUTRITION
Calories *333*; Sugars *8 g*; Protein *12 g*;
Carbohydrate *43 g*; Fat *14 g*; Saturates *4 g*

⭐⭐⭐   moderate

🕐   1 hr

🕐   40 mins

🍳 **COOK'S TIP**

Prosciutto is an Italian, dry-cured, raw ham, said by many to be the best in the world. Other famous varieties of prosciutto include San Daniele and Veneto. This pizza would also be delicious made with Virginian Smithfield ham.

This pizza is made with a dough base flavored with cheese and topped with a delicious tomato sauce and roasted bell peppers.

Tomato Sauce *and* Bell Peppers

1 Sift the flour into a bowl. Add the butter and rub it in with your fingertips until the mixture resembles bread crumbs. Stir in the salt and the Parmesan cheese. Add the egg and 1 tablespoon of the water and mix with a round-bladed knife. Add more water if necessary to make a soft dough. Form into a ball, cover with plastic wrap and let chill in the refrigerator for 30 minutes.

2 Meanwhile, heat the olive oil in a skillet over low heat. Add the onions and garlic and cook for about 5 minutes or until golden. Add the tomatoes and cook for 8–10 minutes. Stir in the tomato paste.

3 Place the bell pepper, skin side up, on a cookie sheet and cook under a preheated hot broiler for 15 minutes until charred. Place in a plastic bag and let sweat for 10 minutes. Peel off the skin and slice the flesh into thin strips.

4 Roll out the dough to fit a 9-inch/23-cm loose-bottom fluted tart pan. Line with foil and bake in a preheated oven, 400°F/200°C, for 10 minutes or until just set. Remove the foil and bake for another 5 minutes until lightly golden. Let cool slightly.

5 Spoon the tomato sauce evenly over the dough and top with the bell pepper strips, thyme, olives, and fresh Parmesan cheese. Return to the oven for about 15 minutes or until the dough is crisp. Serve warm or cold.

SERVES 4

generous 1½ cups all-purpose flour
1 cup butter, diced
½ tsp salt
scant ½ cup dried grated Parmesan cheese
1 egg, beaten
2 tbsp water
2 tbsp olive oil
1 large onion, chopped finely
1 garlic clove, chopped
14 oz/400 g canned chopped tomatoes
4 tbsp concentrated tomato paste
1 red bell pepper, halved
5 fresh thyme sprigs, stalks removed
6 black olives, pitted, and halved
⅓ cup freshly grated Parmesan cheese

NUTRITION
Calories *611*; Sugars *8 g*; Protein *14 g*;
Carbohydrate *56 g*; Fat *38 g*; Saturates *21 g*

⊛⊛⊛   moderate

☺   1 hr 30 mins

🕑   55 mins

This traditional Easter risotto pie is from Piedmont in northern Italy. Cut into slices and serve it either warm or cold.

Green Easter Pie

SERVES 4

1 tbsp butter, for greasing
3 oz/85 g arugula (about 1½ bunches)
2 tbsp olive oil
1 onion, chopped
2 garlic cloves, chopped
7 oz/200 g risotto rice
scant 3 cups hot chicken or vegetable
    bouillon
scant ½ cup white wine
scant ⅔ cup freshly grated Parmesan cheese
1 cup frozen peas, thawed
2 tomatoes, diced
4 eggs, beaten
3 tbsp chopped fresh marjoram
1 cup fresh bread crumbs
salt and pepper

1 Lightly grease a 9-inch/23-cm deep cake pan with butter and line with baking parchment. Using a sharp knife, coarsely chop the arugula.

2 Heat the olive oil in a large skillet over low heat. Add the onion and garlic and cook for 4–5 minutes or until softened.

3 Add the rice to the mixture in the skillet, mix well, then start adding the bouillon, a ladleful at a time. Wait until each ladleful of the bouillon has been absorbed before adding the next.

4 Continue to cook the mixture, adding the wine, until the rice is tender. This will take at least 15 minutes. Remove the skillet from the heat.

5 Stir in the Parmesan cheese, peas, arugula, tomatoes, eggs, and 2 tablespoons of the marjoram. Season to taste with salt and pepper.

6 Spoon the risotto into the prepared pan and smooth the surface by pressing down with the back of a wooden spoon. Top with the bread crumbs and the remaining marjoram.

7 Bake in a preheated oven, 350°F/180°C, for 30 minutes or until set. Cut into slices and serve.

NUTRITION
Calories 392; Sugars 3 g; Protein 17 g;
Carbohydrate 41 g; Fat 17 g; Saturates 5 g

⭐⭐⭐   moderate

🕐   25 mins

🕐   50 mins

This puff pastry pie looks extremely impressive, but it is actually fairly easy to make. Serve it hot or cold.

Spinach *and* Ricotta Pie

1 Rinse the spinach, place in a large pan with just the water clinging to the leaves and cook over low heat for 4–5 minutes until wilted. Drain well. When the spinach is cool enough to handle, squeeze out the excess liquid.

2 Place the pine nuts on a cookie sheet and lightly toast under a preheated hot broiler for 2–3 minutes or until golden-brown.

3 Mix the ricotta, spinach, and eggs together in a bowl. Add the pine nuts, beat well, then stir in the ground almonds and Parmesan cheese.

4 Roll out the puff pie dough on a lightly floured surface and make 2 squares about 8 inches/20 cm wide. Trim the edges, reserving the pastry trimmings.

5 Place 1 dough square on a cookie sheet and spoon the spinach mixture on top, keeping within ½ inch/1 cm of the edge of the square. Brush the edges with beaten egg and place the second square over the top.

6 Using a round-bladed knife, press the edges together by tapping along the sealed edge. Use the pie dough trimmings to make a few leaves to decorate the pie.

7 Brush the pie with the beaten egg and bake in a preheated oven, 425°F/220°C, for 10 minutes. Reduce the oven temperature to 375°F/190°C and bake for another 25–30 minutes. Serve hot.

SERVES 4

8 oz/225 g fresh spinach
¼ cup pine nuts
½ cup ricotta cheese
2 large eggs, beaten
scant ½ cup ground almonds
½ cup freshly grated Parmesan cheese
9 oz/250 g puff pie dough, thawed if frozen
all-purpose flour, for dusting
1 small egg, beaten

NUTRITION
Calories *545*; Sugars *3 g*; Protein *19 g*;
Carbohydrate *25 g*; Fat *42 g*; Saturates *13 g*

⭐⭐⭐   moderate
🕐   25 mins
🕐   50 mins

Always check the seasoning of vegetables—you can always add a little more to a recipe, but you cannot take it out once it has been added.

Spinach *and* Mushroom Lasagna

SERVES 4

½ cup butter, plus extra for greasing
2 garlic cloves, chopped finely
4 oz/115 g shallots
8 oz/225 g exotic mushrooms, such as chanterelles
1 lb/450 g spinach, cooked, drained, and finely chopped
2 cups grated sharp cheese
¼ tsp freshly grated nutmeg
1 tsp chopped fresh basil
scant ½ cup all-purpose flour
2½ cups hot milk
⅔ cup grated mellow hard cheese
8 sheets precooked lasagna
salt and pepper
salad greens, to serve

1 Lightly grease a large ovenproof dish with butter.

2 Melt 4 tablespoons of the butter in a skillet over low heat. Add the garlic, shallots, and exotic mushrooms and cook, stirring frequently, for 3 minutes.

3 Stir in the spinach, sharp cheese, nutmeg, and basil. Season to taste with salt and pepper and set aside.

4 Melt the remaining butter in a small pan over low heat. Add the flour and cook, stirring constantly, for 1 minute. Gradually stir in the hot milk, whisking constantly until smooth. Stir in ¼ cup of the mellow hard cheese. remove from the heat and season to taste with salt and pepper.

5 Spread half of the mushroom and spinach mixture over the bottom of the prepared dish. Cover with a layer of lasagna and then with half of the cheese sauce. Repeat the layers and sprinkle the remaining mellow hard cheese over the top.

6 Bake in a preheated oven, at 400°F/200°C, for about 30 minutes or until the topping is golden-brown and bubbling. Serve hot with salad greens.

NUTRITION
Calories 720; Sugars 9 g; Protein 31 g;
Carbohydrate 36 g; Fat 52 g; Saturates 32 g

easy
20 mins
40 mins

COOK'S TIP

You could substitute 4 bell peppers for the spinach. Roast in a preheated oven, at 400°F/200°C, for 20 minutes. Rub off the skins under cold water, seed, and chop before using.

It is important not to overcook the vegetable filling or it will become sloppy and unexciting, instead of firm to the bite and delicious.

Vegetable Ravioli

1 To make the stuffing, cut the eggplants and zucchini into 1-inch/2.5-cm chunks. Place the eggplant pieces in layers in a strainer, sprinkle each layer with salt and set aside for 20 minutes. Rinse and drain, then pat dry on paper towels.

2 Blanch the tomatoes in boiling water for 2 minutes. Drain, peel, and chop the flesh. Core and seed the bell peppers and cut into 1-inch/2.5-cm dice. Chop the garlic and onion.

3 Heat the olive oil in a pan over low heat. Add the garlic and onion and cook, stirring occasionally, for 3 minutes. Stir in the eggplants, zucchini, tomatoes, bell peppers, tomato paste, and basil. Season to taste with salt and pepper, cover and let simmer for 20 minutes, stirring frequently.

4 Roll out the dough on a lightly floured surface and cut out 3-inch/7.5-cm circles with a plain cutter. Put a spoonful of the vegetable stuffing on each circle. Dampen the edges slightly and fold the pasta circles over, pressing together to seal.

5 Bring a large pan of lightly salted water to a boil over medium heat. Add the ravioli and the olive oil, bring back to a boil, and cook for about 3–4 minutes. Drain and transfer to a greased ovenproof dish, dotting each layer with butter. Pour over the cream and sprinkle over the Parmesan cheese. Bake in a preheated oven, 400°F/200°C, for 20 minutes. Garnish with a few sprigs of basil and serve hot.

SERVES 4

1 lb/450 g Basic Pasta Dough (see page 15)
all-purpose flour, for dusting
1 tbsp olive oil
6 tbsp butter, plus extra for greasing
²⁄₃ cup light cream
³⁄₄ cup freshly grated Parmesan cheese
fresh basil sprigs, to garnish

stuffing
2 large eggplants
3 large zucchini
6 large tomatoes
1 large green bell pepper
1 large red bell pepper
3 garlic cloves
1 large onion
¹⁄₂ cup olive oil
2 tbsp tomato paste
¹⁄₂ tsp chopped fresh basil
salt and pepper

NUTRITION
Calories *622*; Sugars *10 g*; Protein *12 g*;
Carbohydrate *58 g*; Fat *40 g*; Saturates *6 g*

★★★★ challenging
        1 hr 30 mins
        55 mins

This rich, baked pasta dish is packed full of flavorsome vegetables, tomatoes, and Italian mozzarella cheese.

Vegetable Lasagna

SERVES 6

2 large or 3 medium eggplants,
   about 2 lb 4 oz/1 kg total weight
½ cup olive oil
2 tbsp garlic and herb butter
1 lb/450 g zucchini, sliced
2 cups grated mozzarella cheese
2½ cups strained tomatoes
6 sheets precooked green lasagna
2½ cups Béchamel Sauce (see page 73)
⅔ cup freshly grated Parmesan cheese
1 tsp dried oregano
salt and pepper

NUTRITION
Calories 510; Sugars 14 g; Protein 17 g;
Carbohydrate 28 g; Fat 38 g; Saturates 14 g

⭐⭐⭐   moderate
🕐   50 mins
🕐   50 mins

1 Thinly slice the eggplants and place in layers in a strainer. Sprinkle each layer with salt and set aside for 20 minutes. Rinse under cold water and drain, then pat dry on paper towels.

2 Heat 4 tablespoons of the olive oil in a large skillet over low heat. Add half of the eggplant slices and cook for 6–7 minutes or until golden. Drain thoroughly on paper towels. Repeat with the remaining olive oil and eggplant slices.

3 Melt the garlic and herb butter in the skillet over medium heat. Add the zucchini and cook, stirring frequently, for 5–6 minutes until golden-brown all over. Drain thoroughly on paper towels.

4 Place half of the eggplant and half of the zucchini slices in a large ovenproof dish. Season to taste with pepper and sprinkle over half of the mozzarella cheese. Spoon over half of the strained tomatoes and top with 3 sheets of lasagna. Repeat the layering process, ending with a layer of lasagna.

5 Spoon over the béchamel sauce and sprinkle over the Parmesan cheese and oregano. Put the dish on a cookie sheet and bake in a preheated oven, 425°F/220°C, for 30–35 minutes, or until golden-brown. Serve immediately straight from the dish.

Combined with tomatoes and mozzarella cheese, pasta makes a tasty filling for baked eggplant shells.

Filled Eggplants

1 Bring a large pan of lightly salted water to a boil over medium heat. Add the penne and 1 tablespoon of the olive oil, bring back to a boil, and cook for 8–10 minutes or until tender, but still firm to the bite. Drain, return to the pan, cover, and keep warm.

2 Cut the eggplants in half lengthwise and score around the inside with a sharp knife, being careful not to pierce the shells. Scoop out the flesh with a spoon, then brush the insides of the shells with olive oil. Chop the flesh and set aside.

3 Heat the remaining olive oil in a skillet over medium heat. Add the onion and cook until translucent. Add the garlic and cook for 1 minute. Add the chopped eggplant flesh and cook, stirring frequently, for 5 minutes. Add the tomatoes and oregano and season to taste with salt and pepper. Bring to a boil and let simmer for 10 minutes or until thickened. Remove the skillet from the heat and stir in the pasta.

4 Brush a cookie sheet with olive oil and arrange the eggplant shells in a single layer. Divide half of the tomato and pasta mixture among them. Sprinkle over the mozzarella cheese, then pile the remaining tomato and pasta mixture on top. Mix the Parmesan cheese and bread crumbs together and sprinkle over the top, patting it lightly into the mixture.

5 Bake in a preheated oven, 400°C/200°C, for about 25 minutes or until the topping is golden-brown. Serve hot with salad greens.

SERVES 4

8 oz/225 g dried penne or other short pasta shapes
4 tbsp olive oil, plus extra for brushing
2 eggplants
1 large onion, chopped
2 garlic cloves, crushed
14 oz/400 g canned chopped tomatoes
2 tsp dried oregano
2 oz/55 g mozzarella cheese, sliced thinly
1/3 cup freshly grated Parmesan cheese
2 tbsp dry bread crumbs
salt and pepper
salad greens, to serve

NUTRITION
Calories 342; Sugars 6 g; Protein 11 g; Carbohydrate 40 g; Fat 16 g; Saturates 4 g

⭐⭐⭐ moderate
🕐 25 mins
🕐 55 mins

This adaptation of an 18th-century Italian dish is baked until it is golden-brown and sizzling, then cut into wedges, like a cake.

Macaroni *and* Shrimp Bake

SERVES 4

12 oz/350 g dried short pasta, such as short-cut macaroni
1 tbsp olive oil, plus extra for brushing
6 tbsp butter, plus extra for greasing
2 small fennel bulbs, sliced thinly, leaves reserved
2½ cups thinly sliced mushrooms
6 oz/175 g cooked, peeled and deveined shrimp, thawed if frozen
2½ cups Béchamel Sauce (see page 73)
cayenne pepper
⅔ cup freshly grated Parmesan cheese
2 large tomatoes, sliced
1 tsp dried oregano
salt
fresh Italian parsley sprigs, to garnish

NUTRITION
Calories *576*; Sugars *6 g*; Protein *25 g*;
Carbohydrate *42 g*; Fat *35 g*; Saturates *19 g*

⊛⊛⊛ moderate
🕐 20 mins
🕐 1 hr 5 mins

1 Bring a large pan of lightly salted water to a boil over medium heat. Add the pasta with 1 tablespoon of olive oil, bring back to a boil and cook for about 8–10 minutes or until tender, but still firm to the bite. Drain, return to the pan, and dot with 2 tablespoons of the butter. Shake the pan well to coat the pasta, cover, and keep warm.

2 Melt the remaining butter in a pan over medium heat. Add the fennel and cook for 3–4 minutes, until it starts to soften. Stir in the mushrooms and cook, stirring constantly, for 2 minutes. Stir in the shrimp, remove the pan from the heat, and set aside until required.

3 Make the béchamel sauce and season with a pinch of cayenne. Remove the pan from the heat and stir in the reserved vegetables and shrimp mixture and the pasta.

4 Grease a round, shallow ovenproof dish. Pour in the pasta mixture and spread evenly. Sprinkle with Parmesan cheese and arrange the tomato slices in a ring around the edge of the dish. Brush the tomato slices with olive oil and sprinkle with the dried oregano.

5 Bake in a preheated oven, 350°F/180°C, for 25 minutes, or until golden-brown. Transfer to 4 warmed serving plates, garnish with sprigs of fresh parsley, and serve hot.

You can use any fish and any sauce you like in this recipe: try smoked haddock and whiskey sauce or cod with cheese sauce.

Seafood Lasagna

1 Put the haddock fillet, shrimp, and sole fillet into a large bowl and season with pepper and lemon juice according to taste. Set aside while you make the sauce.

2 Melt the butter in a large pan over low heat. Add the leeks and cook, stirring occasionally, for about 8 minutes until softened. Add the flour and cook, stirring constantly, for 1 minute. Gradually stir in enough milk to make a thick, creamy sauce.

3 Blend in the honey and mozzarella cheese and cook for another 3 minutes. Remove the pan from the heat and mix in the fish and shrimp.

4 Grease a large ovenproof dish with butter. Make alternate layers of fish sauce and lasagna, finishing with a layer of fish sauce on top. Sprinkle over the Parmesan cheese and bake in a preheated oven, 350°F/180°C, for about 30 minutes or until golden-brown. Serve immediately.

SERVES 4

1 lb/450 g haddock, filleted, skin removed and flesh flaked
4 oz/115 g raw shrimp, peeled and deveined
4 oz/115 g sole fillet, skin removed and flesh sliced
juice of 1 lemon
4 tbsp butter, plus extra for greasing
3 leeks, sliced very thinly
scant ½ cup all-purpose flour
2⅓ cups milk
2 tbsp honey
2 cups grated mozzarella cheese
1 lb/450 g precooked lasagna
⅔ cup freshly grated Parmesan cheese
pepper

NUTRITION
Calories 790; Sugars 23 g; Protein 55 g; Carbohydrate 74 g; Fat 32 g; Saturates 19 g

✪✪✪   moderate
🕐   30 mins
🕐   45 mins

🍳 **COOK'S TIP**

To make a hard cider sauce, substitute 1 finely chopped shallot for the leeks, 1½ cups cider and 1½ cups heavy cream for the milk, and 1 teaspoon of mustard for the honey.

This flavorsome and colorful fish pie is perfect for a light meal. The addition of smoked salmon gives it a touch of luxury.

Smoky Fish Pie

SERVES 4

2 lb/900 g smoked haddock or cod fillets

2½ cups skim milk

2 bay leaves

4 oz/115 g white mushrooms, cut into fourths

1 cup frozen peas

⅔ cup frozen corn kernels

4 cups diced potatoes

5 tbsp lowfat plain yogurt

4 tbsp chopped fresh parsley

2 oz/55 g smoked salmon, sliced into thin strips

3 tbsp cornstarch

¼ cup grated smoked cheese

salt and pepper

NUTRITION

Calories 523; Sugars 15 g; Protein 58 g; Carbohydrate 63 g; Fat 6 g; Saturates 2 g

moderate

15 mins

1 hr

1 Place the fish in a large skillet and add the milk and bay leaves. Bring to a boil over medium heat, cover, and let simmer gently for 5 minutes. Add the mushrooms, peas, and corn, bring back to a simmer, cover, and cook for about 5–7 minutes. Let cool.

2 Place the potatoes in a pan, cover with water, bring to a boil over medium heat, and cook for 8 minutes. Drain well and mash with a fork. Stir in the yogurt and parsley, then season to taste with salt and pepper. Set aside.

3 Using a draining spoon, remove the fish from the pan. Flake the cooked fish away from the skin and place in an ovenproof dish. Set aside the cooking liquid. Drain the vegetables and set aside the cooking liquid. Gently stir the vegetables into the fish with the salmon strips.

4 Blend the cornstarch with a little cooking liquid to make a paste. Transfer the rest of the liquid to a pan and add the paste. Heat through, stirring, until thickened. Remove and discard the bay leaves and season to taste. Pour the sauce over the fish and vegetables and mix. Spoon over the mashed potato to cover, sprinkle with the grated cheese, and bake in a preheated oven, 400°F/200°C, for 25–30 minutes. Serve hot.

COOK'S TIP

If possible, use smoked haddock or cod that has not been dyed bright yellow or artificially flavored to give the illusion of having been smoked.

This dish is ideal for a substantial meal. You can use whatever pasta you like, but the tricolor varieties will give the most colorful results.

Shrimp Pasta Bake

1 Bring a large pan of lightly salted water to a boil over medium heat. Add the pasta, bring back to a boil, and cook for 8–10 minutes until tender, but still firm to the bite. Drain well and set aside.

2 Meanwhile, heat the vegetable oil in a small skillet over low heat. Add the mushrooms and all but a handful of the scallions and cook, stirring frequently, for 4–5 minutes until softened.

3 Place the cooked pasta in a bowl and mix in the mushroom and scallion mixture, tuna, and shrimp.

4 Blend the cornstarch with a little milk to make a paste. Pour the remaining milk into a pan and stir in the paste. Heat, stirring constantly, until the sauce starts to thicken. Season well with salt and pepper. Add the sauce to the pasta mixture and mix thoroughly. Transfer to an ovenproof dish and place on a cookie sheet.

5 Place the tomato slices over the pasta and sprinkle with the bread crumbs and cheese. Bake in a preheated oven, 375°F/190°C, for about 25–30 minutes or until golden-brown. Sprinkle with the reserved scallions and serve hot.

SERVES 4

8 oz/225 g dried tricolor pasta shapes
1 tbsp vegetable oil
2½ cups sliced white mushrooms
1 bunch scallions, trimmed and chopped
14 oz/400 g canned tuna in brine, drained
    and flaked
6 oz/175 g peeled and deveined shrimp,
    thawed if frozen
2 tbsp cornstarch
1¾ cups skim milk
4 tomatoes, sliced thinly
½ cup fresh bread crumbs
¼ cup grated reduced-fat colby cheese
salt and pepper

NUTRITION

Calories *723*; Sugars *9 g*; Protein *56 g*;
Carbohydrate *114 g*; Fat *8 g*; Saturates *2 g*

challenging

10 mins

50 mins

Using cornmeal as a crust for a gratin dish gives a lovely crispy outer texture and a smooth inside. It works well with smoked fish and chicken.

Smoked Cod Cornmeal

SERVES 4

6½ cups water
generous 2⅓ cups instant cornmeal
7 oz/200 g chopped frozen spinach, thawed
3 tbsp butter
½ cup grated romano cheese
generous ¾ cup milk
1 lb/450 g smoked cod fillet, skinned and
    boned
4 eggs, beaten
salt and pepper

1 Bring the water to a boil in a large pan over medium heat. Add the cornmeal and cook, stirring constantly, for 30–35 minutes.

2 Stir the spinach, butter, and half of the romano cheese into the cornmeal. Season to taste with salt and pepper.

3 Divide the cooked cornmeal mixture among 4 individual ovenproof dishes, spreading it evenly across the bottom and up the sides of the dishes.

4 Bring the milk to a boil in a large skillet over low heat. Add the fish and cook gently, turning once, for 8–10 minutes or until the flesh is tender and flakes easily when tested with a fork. Remove the fish with a draining spoon.

5 Remove the skillet from the heat. Pour the eggs into the milk in the skillet and mix together.

6 Using a fork, flake the fish into smaller pieces and place it in the center of the dishes, then pour the milk and egg mixture over the fish.

7 Sprinkle with the remaining cheese and bake in a preheated oven, 375°F/190°C, for 25–30 minutes or until set and golden. Serve hot.

NUTRITION
Calories 616; Sugars 3 g; Protein 41 g;
Carbohydrate 58 g; Fat 24 g; Saturates 12 g

moderate
30 mins
1 hr 15 mins

🍳 **COOK'S TIP**

Try using 12 oz/350 g cooked chicken breast with 2 tablespoons of chopped fresh tarragon, instead of the smoked cod, if you prefer.

Cod roasted with herbs and topped with a lemon and rosemary crust is a delicious main course for a warm summer evening.

Italian Cod

1 Melt the butter in a large pan over low heat.

2 Remove the pan from the heat and add the bread crumbs, walnuts, the peel and juice of 1 lemon, half of the rosemary, and half of the parsley.

3 Gently press the bread crumb mixture over the top of the cod fillets. Place the cod fillets in a shallow, foil-lined roasting pan.

4 Bake in a preheated oven, 400°F/200°C, for 25–30 minutes.

5 Mix the garlic, the remaining lemon peel and juice, rosemary, parsley, and the chile together in a bowl. Beat in the walnut oil and mix well. Drizzle the dressing over the cod steaks as soon as they are cooked.

6 Transfer the fish to 4 serving plates and serve with salad greens.

SERVES 4

2 tbsp butter
1 cup fresh whole-wheat bread crumbs
2 tbsp chopped walnuts
grated peel and juice of 2 lemons
2 sprigs fresh rosemary sprigs, stems removed
2 tbsp chopped fresh parsley
4 cod fillets, about 5½ oz/150 g each
1 garlic clove, crushed
1 small fresh red chile, seeded and diced
3 tbsp walnut oil
salad greens, to serve

NUTRITION
Calories *313*; Sugars *0.4 g*; Protein *29 g*; Carbohydrate *6 g*; Fat *20 g*; Saturates *5 g*

⊕⊕ easy
🕐 10 mins
🕐 35 mins

🍽 **COOK'S TIP**

If preferred, the walnuts may be omitted from the crust. In addition, extra virgin olive oil can be used instead of walnut oil, if you prefer.

This is a lighter dish than the better-known cannelloni stuffed with ground beef and would be a good choice for an informal dinner party.

Cannelloni Filetti *di* Sogliola

SERVES 6

12 small sole fillets, about 4 oz/115 g each
²⁄₃ cup red wine
6 tbsp butter
1²⁄₃ cups sliced white mushrooms
4 shallots, chopped finely
4 oz/115 g tomatoes, chopped
2 tbsp tomato paste
scant ½ cup all-purpose flour, strained
²⁄₃ cup warm milk
2 tbsp heavy cream
6 dried cannelloni tubes
6 oz/175 g cooked, peeled and deveined
    shrimp, preferably freshwater
salt and pepper
1 fresh fennel frond, to garnish

NUTRITION
Calories *555*; Sugars *4 g*; Protein *53 g*;
Carbohydrate *36 g*; Fat *2 g*; Saturates *12 g*

⭐⭐⭐⭐ challenging
🕐 20 mins
🕐 45 mins

1 Brush the sole fillets with a little wine, season with salt and pepper and roll them up, skin side inward. Secure with a toothpick.

2 Place the fish rolls in a single layer in a large skillet, add the remaining red wine, and poach for 4 minutes. Remove the fish from the skillet and set aside the liquid.

3 Melt the butter in another skillet over low heat. Add the mushrooms and shallots and cook for 2 minutes, then add the tomatoes and tomato paste. Season the flour and stir it into the skillet. Stir in the reserved cooking liquid and half the milk. Cook, stirring constantly, for 4 minutes. Remove from the heat and stir in the cream.

4 Bring a large pan of lightly salted water to a boil over medium heat. Add the cannelloni tubes, bring back to a boil, and cook for about 8 minutes or until tender but still firm to the bite. Drain and let cool.

5 Remove the toothpicks from the fish rolls. Put 2 sole fillets into each cannelloni tube with 2–3 shrimp and a little red wine sauce. Arrange the cannelloni in a single layer in an ovenproof dish, pour over the sauce and bake in a preheated oven, 400°F/200°C, for 20 minutes.

6 Serve the cannelloni with the red wine sauce, garnished with the remaining shrimp and a frond of fresh fennel.

This simple recipe perfectly complements the exceptionally sweet flavor and delicate texture of the fish.

Fillets *of* Snapper *and* Pasta

1 Place the red snapper fillets in a large casserole. Pour over the wine and add the shallots, garlic, herbs, lemon zest and juice, nutmeg, and anchovies. Season to taste with salt and pepper. Cover and bake in a preheated oven, 350°F/180°C, for 35 minutes.

2 Transfer the red snapper to a warmed dish. Set aside and keep warm.

3 Pour the cooking liquid into a pan and bring to a boil over medium heat. Let simmer gently for 25 minutes or until reduced by half. Mix the cream and cornstarch together and stir into the sauce to thicken.

4 Meanwhile, bring a large pan of lightly salted water to a boil over medium heat. Add the vermicelli and olive oil, bring back to a boil, and cook for about 8–10 minutes or until tender but still firm to the bite. Drain the pasta and transfer to 4 warmed serving dishes.

5 Arrange the red snapper fillets on top of the vermicelli and pour over the sauce. Garnish with fresh mint sprigs, slices of lemon, and strips of lemon peel, and serve immediately.

SERVES 4

2 lb 4 oz/1 kg red snapper fillets
1¼ cups dry white wine
4 shallots, chopped finely
1 garlic clove, crushed
3 tbsp finely chopped mixed fresh herbs
finely grated zest and juice of 1 lemon
pinch of freshly grated nutmeg
3 anchovy fillets, chopped coarsely
2 tbsp heavy cream
1 tsp cornstarch
1 lb/450 g dried vermicelli
1 tbsp olive oil
salt and pepper

to garnish
1 fresh mint sprig
lemon slices
strips of lemon peel

NUTRITION
Calories *457*; Sugars *3 g*; Protein *39 g*; Carbohydrate *44 g*; Fat *12 g*; Saturates *5 g*

✪✪✪   moderate

    15 mins

    1 hr

Most trout available nowadays is farmed rainbow trout, however, if you can, buy the marvelous-tasting wild brown trout for this recipe.

Trout *with* Smoked Bacon

SERVES 4

1 tbsp butter, for greasing
4 whole trout, about 9½ oz/275 g each, cleaned and rinsed
12 anchovies in oil, drained and chopped
2 apples, peeled, cored, and sliced
4 fresh mint sprigs
juice of 1 lemon
12 slices smoked fatty bacon
1 lb/450 g dried tagliatelle
1 tbsp olive oil
salt and pepper

to garnish
2 apples, cored and sliced
4 fresh mint sprigs

1 Grease a deep cookie sheet with the butter.

2 Open up the cavities of each trout and rinse with warm salt water.

3 Season each cavity with salt and pepper. Divide the anchovies, sliced apples, and mint sprigs among the cavities. Sprinkle with the lemon juice.

4 Cover the whole of each trout, except the head and tail, with 3 slices of smoked bacon in a spiral.

5 Arrange the trout on the prepared cookie sheet with the loose ends of bacon tucked underneath. Season to taste with pepper and bake in a preheated oven, 400°F/200°C, for 20 minutes, turning the trout over after 10 minutes.

6 Meanwhile, bring a large pan of lightly salted water to a boil over medium heat. Add the tagliatelle and olive oil, bring back to a boil and cook for about 12 minutes or until tender, but still firm to the bite. Drain and transfer to a large, warmed serving dish.

7 Remove the trout from the oven and arrange on the tagliatelle. Garnish with sliced apples and fresh mint sprigs and serve immediately.

NUTRITION
Calories *802*; Sugars *8 g*; Protein *68 g*;
Carbohydrate *54 g*; Fat *36 g*; Saturates *10 g*

✪✪✪✪   challenging
◔   35 mins
⏱   30 mins

This quick, easy, and inexpensive dish would be ideal for a mid-week family meal and will quickly become a firm favorite.

Smoked Haddock Casserole

1 Grease a large casserole with butter. Place the haddock in the casserole and pour over the milk. Bake in a preheated oven, 400°F/200°C, for 15 minutes until the flesh is tender and flakes easily with a fork. Carefully pour the cooking liquid into a pitcher without breaking up the fish.

2 Melt the butter in a pan over low heat and stir in the flour. Gradually whisk in the reserved cooking liquid. Season to taste with salt, pepper, and nutmeg. Stir in the cream, parsley, and mashed hard-cooked egg and cook, stirring constantly, for 2 minutes.

3 Meanwhile, bring a large pan of lightly salted water to a boil over medium heat. Add the fusilli and lemon juice, bring back to a boil, and cook for about 8–10 minutes or until tender, but still firm to the bite.

4 Drain the pasta and spoon or tip it over the fish. Top with the egg sauce and return the casserole to the oven for 10 minutes.

5 Transfer the casserole to 4 warmed serving plates and garnish with sprigs of fresh parsley. Serve with boiled new potatoes and beet.

SERVES 4

2 tbsp butter, plus extra for greasing
1 lb/450 g smoked haddock fillets, cut into 4 slices
2½ cups milk
scant ¼ cup all-purpose flour
pinch of freshly grated nutmeg
3 tbsp heavy cream
1 tbsp chopped fresh parsley
2 eggs, hard-cooked and mashed to a pulp
4 cups dried fusilli
1 tbsp lemon juice
salt and pepper
fresh Italian parsley sprigs, to garnish

to serve
boiled new potatoes
freshly cooked beet

NUTRITION
Calories *525*; Sugars *8 g*; Protein *41 g*;
Carbohydrate *53 g*; Fat *18 g*; Saturates *10 g*

⭐⭐⭐   moderate
🕐   20 mins
🕐   45 mins

COOK'S TIP

You can use any type of dried pasta for this casserole. Try penne, conchiglie, farfalle, or rigatoni.

This recipe is a type of cottage pie and is just as versatile. Add vegetables and herbs of your choice, depending on what you have at hand.

Quick Chicken Bake

SERVES 4

1 lb 2 oz/500 g ground chicken
1 large onion, chopped finely
2 carrots, diced finely
¼ cup all-purpose flour
1 tbsp tomato paste
1¼ cups chicken bouillon
pinch of fresh thyme
2 lb/900 g boiled potatoes, creamed with
    butter and milk and highly seasoned
¾ cup grated Lancashire or sharp cheese
salt and pepper
freshly cooked peas, to serve

1 Dry-fry the ground chicken, onion, and carrots in a non-stick pan over low heat for 5 minutes, stirring frequently.

2 Sprinkle the chicken with the flour and let simmer for another 2 minutes.

3 Gradually blend in the tomato paste and bouillon, then let simmer gently for 15 minutes. Season to taste with salt and pepper and add the thyme.

4 Transfer the chicken and vegetable mixture to a casserole and let cool.

5 Spoon the mashed potato over the chicken mixture and sprinkle with the grated cheese. Bake in a preheated oven, 400°F/200°C, for 20 minutes or until the topping is golden and bubbling. Serve with freshly cooked peas.

NUTRITION
Calories 530; Sugars 8 g; Protein 37 g;
Carbohydrate 48 g; Fat 23 g; Saturates 12 g

moderate

1 hr 45 mins

45 mins

🍳 **COOK'S TIP**

Instead of Lancashire or sharp cheese, you could sprinkle Fresh Jack, Plymouth cheese, or even Toscana over the top, if available.

This cooking method makes the chicken aromatic and succulent, and reduces the oil needed as the chicken and vegetables cook in their own juices.

Italian Chicken Parcels

1 Cut 6 pieces of foil, each measuring about 10-inches/25-cm square. Brush the foil squares lightly with the olive oil and set aside until required.

2 Using a sharp knife, slash each chicken breast at regular intervals. Cut the mozzarella cheese into slices and place among the cuts in each of the chicken breasts.

3 Divide the zucchini and tomatoes among the pieces of foil and season to taste with pepper. Tear or coarsely chop the basil or oregano and sprinkle over the vegetables in each parcel.

4 Place the chicken on top of each pile of vegetables, then wrap in the foil, tucking in the ends.

5 Place on a cookie sheet and bake in a preheated oven, 400°C/200°C, for about 30 minutes. To serve, unwrap each foil parcel and serve with freshly cooked rice or pasta.

SERVES 4

1 tbsp olive oil
6 skinless chicken breast fillets
9 oz/250 g mozzarella cheese
3½ cups sliced zucchini
6 large tomatoes, sliced
1 small bunch of fresh basil or oregano
pepper
freshly cooked rice or pasta, to serve

NUTRITION
Calories 234; Sugars 5 g; Protein 28 g; Carbohydrate 5 g; Fat 12 g; Saturates 5 g

⊛⊛ easy
☺ 25 mins
☻ 30 mins

COOK'S TIP

To aid cooking, place the vegetables and chicken on the shiny side of the foil so that when the parcel is wrapped the dull surface of the foil is facing outward. This ensures that the heat is absorbed into the parcel.

Chicken breasts are stuffed with ricotta, nutmeg, and spinach, then wrapped with wafer-thin slices of prosciutto and cooked in white wine.

Prosciutto-Wrapped Chicken

SERVES 4

4½ oz/125 g frozen spinach, thawed
¾ cup ricotta cheese
pinch of freshly grated nutmeg
4 skinless, boneless chicken breasts, about
   6 oz/175 g each
4 prosciutto slices
2 tbsp butter
1 tbsp olive oil
12 small onions or shallots
2 cups sliced white mushrooms
1 tbsp all-purpose flour
⅔ cup dry white or red wine
1¼ cups chicken bouillon
salt and pepper

to serve
carrot purée
freshly cooked green beans

NUTRITION
Calories *426*; Sugars *4 g*; Protein *44 g*;
Carbohydrate *9 g*; Fat *21 g*; Saturates *8 g*

✪✪✪   moderate
🕐   30 mins
🕐   45 mins

1 Place the spinach in a strainer and press out the water with a spoon. Mix with the ricotta and nutmeg and season to taste with salt and pepper.

2 Using a sharp knife, slit each chicken breast through the side and enlarge each cut to form a pocket. Fill with the spinach mixture, reshape the chicken breasts, wrap each breast in a slice of prosciutto, and secure with toothpicks. Cover and let chill in the refrigerator.

3 Heat the butter and olive oil in a large skillet over low heat. Add the chicken breasts and brown for 2 minutes on each side, then transfer to a large, shallow ovenproof dish and keep warm until required.

4 Add the onions and mushrooms to the skillet and cook over medium heat, stirring occasionally, for 2–3 minutes or until lightly browned. Stir in the flour, then gradually stir in the wine and bouillon. Bring to a boil, stirring constantly, and cook until thickened. Season to taste with salt and pepper. Spoon the mixture around the chicken.

5 Cook the chicken, uncovered, in a preheated oven, 400°F/200°C, for about 20 minutes. Turn the chicken breasts over and cook for another 10 minutes. Remove the toothpicks and serve the chicken with the sauce, carrot purée, and freshly cooked green beans.

These little foil parcels retain all the natural juices of the chicken, making a superb and delicious sauce for the pasta.

Italian Chicken Spirals

1 Beat the chicken breasts with a rolling pin to flatten evenly.

2 Place the basil and hazelnuts in a food processor and process until finely chopped. Mix with the garlic and salt and pepper to taste.

3 Spread the basil mixture over the chicken breasts and roll up from a short end to enclose the filling. Wrap the chicken rolls tightly in foil so they hold their shape, then seal the ends well. Place the rolls on a cookie sheet and bake in a preheated oven 400°F/200°C, for 20–25 minutes

4 Meanwhile, bring a large pan of lightly salted water to a boil over medium heat. Add the fusilli, bring back to a boil, and cook for 8–10 minutes or until tender but firm to the bite.

5 Drain the pasta and return to the pan with the lemon juice, olive oil, tomatoes, capers, and olives. Warm through and transfer to a large, warmed serving dish.

6 Check that the chicken is cooked by piercing the rolls with a toothpick or the point of a sharp knife to make sure that the juices run clear. Slice the chicken and arrange over the pasta. Serve immediately.

COOK'S TIP

Sun-dried tomatoes have a wonderful, rich flavor but if they are unavailable, use fresh tomatoes instead.

SERVES 4

4 skinless, boneless chicken breasts
1 cup fresh basil leaves
1 tbsp hazelnuts
1 garlic clove, crushed
9 oz/250 g dried whole-wheat fusilli
2 sun-dried tomatoes or fresh tomatoes, diced
1 tbsp lemon juice
1 tbsp olive oil
1 tbsp capers
½ cup pitted black olives
salt and pepper

NUTRITION
Calories 367; Sugars 1 g; Protein 33 g;
Carbohydrate 35 g; Fat 12 g; Saturates 2 g

⭐⭐⭐ moderate
🕐 20 mins
🕐 40 mins

Chicken pieces are cooked in a succulent, mild mustard sauce, then coated in poppy seeds, and served on a bed of fresh pasta shells.

Mustard Baked Chicken

SERVES 4

8 chicken pieces, about 4 oz/115 g each
4 tbsp butter, melted
4 tbsp mild mustard (see Cook's Tip)
2 tbsp lemon juice
1 tbsp brown sugar
1 tsp paprika
3 tbsp poppy seeds
14 oz/400 g dried pasta shells
1 tbsp olive oil
salt and pepper
cracked black pepper, to garnish

NUTRITION
Calories *652*; Sugars *5 g*; Protein *51 g*;
Carbohydrate *46 g*; Fat *31 g*; Saturates *12 g*

easy

10 mins

35 mins

1 Arrange the chicken pieces in a single layer in a large ovenproof dish.

2 Mix the butter, mustard, lemon juice, sugar, and paprika together in a bowl and season to taste with salt and pepper. Brush half the mixture over the upper surfaces of the chicken pieces and bake in a preheated oven, 400°F/200°C, for 15 minutes.

3 Remove the dish from the oven and carefully turn the chicken pieces over, using tongs. Coat the upper surfaces of the chicken with the remaining mustard mixture, sprinkle the chicken pieces with the poppy seeds, and return to the oven for another 15 minutes.

4 Meanwhile, bring a large pan of lightly salted water to a boil over medium heat. Add the pasta shells and olive oil, bring back to a boil, and cook for 8–10 minutes or until tender but still firm to the bite.

5 Drain the pasta thoroughly and arrange on 4 warmed serving dishes. Top the pasta with 1 or 2 chicken pieces, pour over the mustard sauce, and garnish with cracked pepper. Serve immediately.

COOK'S TIP

Dijon is the type of mustard most often used in cooking, as it has a clean and only mildly spicy flavor. German mustard has a sweet-sour taste, with Bavarian mustard being slightly sweeter. American mustard is mild and sweet.

Tender lean chicken is baked with pasta in a creamy lowfat sauce which contrasts well with the fennel and the sweetness of the raisins.

Chicken Pasta Bake

1 Trim the fennel and set aside the green fronds. Slice the bulbs thinly.

2 Coat the onions in the lemon juice and cut the mushrooms into fourths.

3 Heat the olive oil in a large skillet over medium heat. Add the fennel, onion, and mushrooms and cook for 4–5 minutes, stirring constantly, until just softened. Season well with salt and pepper and transfer the mixture to a large bowl. Set aside.

4 Bring a large pan of lightly salted water to a boil over medium heat. Add the penne, bring back to a boil, and cook for 8–10 minutes or until tender but still firm to the bite. Drain and mix the pasta with the vegetables.

5 Stir the raisins and chicken into the pasta mixture. Beat the soft cheese to soften, then mix into the pasta and chicken—the heat from the pasta should make the cheese melt slightly.

6 Put the mixture into a large ovenproof dish and place on a cookie sheet. Arrange slices of mozzarella cheese over the top and sprinkle with the grated Parmesan cheese.

7 Bake in a preheated oven, 400°F/200°C, for 20–25 minutes or until golden-brown and the topping is bubbling. Garnish with the reserved fennel fronds and serve hot.

SERVES 4

2 fennel bulbs
2 red onions, shredded finely
1 tbsp lemon juice
4½ oz/125 g white mushrooms
1 tbsp olive oil
8 oz/225 g dried penne
⅓ cup raisins
8 oz/225 g lean, boneless cooked chicken, skinned and shredded
13 oz/375 g lowfat soft cheese with garlic and herbs
4½ oz/125 g lowfat mozzarella cheese, sliced thinly
scant ½ cup freshly grated Parmesan cheese
salt and pepper

NUTRITION
Calories 380; Sugars 15 g; Protein 39 g; Carbohydrate 27 g; Fat 14 g; Saturates 6 g

⭐⭐⭐⭐ challenging
🕐 15 mins
🕐 45 mins

You can use your favorite mushrooms, such as chanterelles or oyster mushrooms, for this delicately flavored dish.

Chicken Lasagna

SERVES 4

1 tbsp butter, for greasing
14 sheets precooked lasagna
3½ cups Béchamel Sauce (see page 73)
¾ cup freshly grated Parmesan cheese

sauce
2 tbsp olive oil
2 garlic cloves, crushed
1 large onion, chopped finely
8 oz/225 g exotic mushrooms, sliced
2½ cups ground chicken
3 oz/85 g chicken livers, chopped finely
¾ cup diced prosciutto
⅔ cup Marsala wine
10 oz/280 g canned chopped tomatoes
1 tbsp chopped fresh basil leaves
2 tbsp tomato paste
salt and pepper

1 To make the sauce, heat the olive oil in a large pan over low heat. Add the garlic, onion, and exotic mushrooms, and cook, stirring frequently, for about 6 minutes.

2 Add the ground chicken, chicken livers, and prosciutto, and cook, stirring frequently, for about 12 minutes or until the meat has browned.

3 Stir the Marsala, tomatoes, basil, and tomato paste into the mixture and cook for 4 minutes. Season to taste with salt and pepper, cover, and let simmer gently for 30 minutes, stirring occasionally. Uncover the pan, stir thoroughly, and let simmer for another 15 minutes.

4 Lightly grease an ovenproof dish with the butter. Arrange sheets of lasagna over the bottom of the dish, spoon over a layer of sauce, then spoon over a layer of béchamel sauce. Place another layer of lasagna on top and repeat the process twice, finishing with a layer of béchamel sauce. Sprinkle over the Parmesan cheese and bake in a preheated oven, 375°F/190°C, for 35 minutes until golden-brown and bubbling. Serve immediately.

NUTRITION
Calories *708*; Sugars *17 g*; Protein *35 g*;
Carbohydrate *57 g*; Fat *35 g*; Saturates *14 g*

✪✪✪✪ challenging
⏱ 40 mins
🕐 1 hr 45 mins

This impressive looking turkey loaf is flavored with herbs and a layer of juicy tomatoes, and covered with zucchini ribbons.

Turkey *and* Vegetable Loaf

1 Line a 2-lb/900-g non-stick loaf pan with baking parchment. Place the onion, garlic, and turkey in a bowl, add the herbs, and season with salt and pepper. Mix together with your hands, then add the egg white to bind.

2 Press half of the turkey mixture into the bottom of the prepared loaf pan. Thinly slice 1 zucchini and the tomatoes and arrange the slices over the meat. Top with the rest of the turkey mixture and press down firmly.

3 Cover with foil and place in a roasting pan. Pour in enough boiling water to come halfway up the sides of the loaf pan. Bake in a preheated oven, 375°F/190°C, for 1–1¼ hours, removing the foil for the last 20 minutes of cooking. Test that the loaf is cooked by inserting a toothpick into the center—the juices should run clear. The loaf will also shrink away from the sides of the pan.

4 Meanwhile, trim the other zucchini. Using a vegetable peeler or hand-held metal cheese slicer, cut the zucchini lengthwise into thin slices. Bring a small pan of water to the boil over medium heat. Add the zucchini ribbons and blanch for 1–2 minutes until just tender. Drain and keep warm.

5 Remove the turkey loaf from the pan and transfer to a warmed serving plate. Drape the zucchini ribbons over the loaf and garnish with sprigs of fresh herbs. Serve immediately.

SERVES 6

1 onion, chopped finely
1 garlic clove, crushed
2 lb/900 g lean ground turkey
1 tbsp chopped fresh parsley
1 tbsp chopped fresh chives
1 tbsp chopped fresh tarragon
1 egg white, beaten lightly
2 zucchini
2 tomatoes
salt and pepper
mixed fresh herbs sprigs, to garnish

NUTRITION
Calories *165*; Sugars *1 g*; Protein *36 g*;
Carbohydrate *1 g*; Fat *2 g*; Saturates *0.5 g*

⭐⭐☆　　　easy

🕐　　　10 mins

🕐　　　1 hr 15 mins

The richness of the duck meat contrasts well with the apricot sauce. If duckling portions are unavailable, use a whole bird cut into portions.

Roast Duck *with* Apple

SERVES 4

4 duckling portions, about 12 oz/350 g each
4 tbsp dark soy sauce
2 tbsp light brown sugar
2 red-skinned apples
2 green-skinned apples
juice of 1 lemon
2 tbsp honey
a few bay leaves
salt and pepper
assorted fresh vegetables, to serve

sauce
14 oz/400 g canned apricots, in natural juice
4 tbsp sweet sherry

1 Wash the duck and trim away any excess fat. Place on a wire rack over a roasting pan and prick all over with a fork or a large needle.

2 Brush the duck with the soy sauce. Sprinkle over the sugar and season to taste with pepper. Cook in a preheated oven, 375°F/190°C, basting occasionally, for 50–60 minutes or until the meat is cooked through—the juices should run clear when a toothpick or the point of a sharp knife is inserted into the thickest part of the meat.

3 Meanwhile, core the apples and cut each into 6 wedges. Place in a small roasting pan and mix with the lemon juice and honey. Add a few bay leaves and season to taste with salt and pepper. Cook alongside the duck, basting occasionally, for 20–25 minutes until tender. Discard the bay leaves.

4 To make the sauce, place the apricots in a blender or food processor with the can juices and sherry. Process for a few seconds until smooth. Alternatively, mash the apricots with a fork and mix with the juices and sherry.

5 Just before serving, heat the apricot sauce in a small pan. Remove the skin from the duck and pat the flesh with paper towels to absorb any fat. Serve the duck with the apple wedges, apricot sauce, and fresh vegetables.

NUTRITION
Calories *316*; Sugars *38 g*; Protein *25 g*;
Carbohydrate *40 g*; Fat *6 g*; Saturates *1 g*

⭐⭐⭐   moderate
🕐   10 mins
🕐   1 hr 30 mins

🍳 COOK'S TIP

Fruit complements duck perfectly. Use canned pineapple in natural juice for a delicious alternative.

Chinese-style duck is very easy to prepare, but makes an impressive main course for a dinner party whatever the occasion.

Honey-Glazed Duck

1 Mix the soy sauce, honey, vinegar, garlic, and star anise together. Blend the cornstarch with the water to form a paste and stir it into the mixture.

2 Place the duck breasts in a large, shallow ovenproof dish. Brush all over with the soy marinade, turning them to coat completely. Cover and let marinate in the refrigerator for at least 2 hours, or overnight.

3 Remove the duck from the marinade and cook in a preheated oven, 425°F/220°C, for 20–25 minutes, basting frequently with the glaze.

4 Remove the duck from the oven and arrange on a broiler rack. Broil under a preheated hot broiler for about 3–4 minutes to caramelize the top.

5 Remove the duck from the broiler pan and cut into fairly thin slices. Arrange the duck slices in a large, warmed serving dish, garnish with celery leaves, cucumber wedges, and chives, and serve immediately.

SERVES 4

1 tsp dark soy sauce
2 tbsp honey
1 tsp white wine vinegar
3 garlic cloves, crushed
1 tsp ground star anise
2 tsp cornstarch
2 tsp water
2 large boneless duckling breasts, about 8 oz/225 g each

to garnish
celery leaves
cucumber wedges
handful of fresh chives

NUTRITION
Calories *230*; Sugars *9 g*; Protein *23 g*; Carbohydrate *14 g*; Fat *9 g*; Saturates *3 g*

⊗⊗   easy
◔   2 hrs 45 mins
⏱   30 mins

🍳 COOK'S TIP

If the duck starts to burn slightly while it is cooking in the oven, cover with foil. Check that the duck breasts are cooked through by inserting the point of a sharp knife into the thickest part of the flesh—the juices should run clear.

In this traditional Chinese dish the pork turns "red" during cooking because it is basted in dark soy sauce.

Red Roast Pork *in* Soy Sauce

SERVES 4

1 lb/450 g lean pork fillets
6 tbsp dark soy sauce
2 tbsp dry sherry
1 tsp Chinese five-spice powder
2 garlic cloves, crushed
2 tsp finely chopped fresh gingerroot
1 large red bell pepper
1 large yellow bell pepper
1 large orange bell pepper
4 tbsp superfine sugar
2 tbsp red wine vinegar

to garnish
shredded scallions
handful of fresh chives

1 Trim away any excess fat and silver skin from the pork and place in a large, shallow dish.

2 Mix the soy sauce, sherry, Chinese five-spice powder, garlic, and ginger together. Spoon the mixture over the pork, turning it to coat, cover, and let marinate in the refrigerator for at least 1 hour or until required.

3 Drain the pork and set aside the marinade. Place the pork on a large roasting rack over a roasting pan. Cook in a preheated oven, 375°F/190°C, basting occasionally with the marinade, for 1 hour or until cooked through.

4 Meanwhile, halve and seed the bell peppers. Cut each bell pepper half into 3 equal pieces. Arrange them on a cookie sheet and bake alongside the pork for the last 30 minutes of the cooking time.

5 Place the sugar and vinegar in a pan and heat until the sugar dissolves. Bring to a boil and let simmer for 3–4 minutes until syrupy.

6 When the pork is cooked, remove it from the oven and brush with the sugar syrup. Let stand for about 5 minutes, then slice, and arrange on a warmed serving plate with the bell peppers and garnish with the scallions and chives. Serve hot.

NUTRITION
Calories *268*; Sugars *20 g*; Protein *26 g*;
Carbohydrate *22 g*; Fat *8 g*; Saturates *3 g*

✪✪✪   moderate
🕐   1 hr 15 mins
🕐   1 hr 15 mins

Cannelloni, the thick, round pasta tubes, make perfect containers for close-textured sauces of all kinds.

Stuffed Cannelloni

1 To make the filling, melt the butter in a pan over low heat. Add the spinach and cook for 2–3 minutes. Remove from the heat and stir in the ricotta and Parmesan cheeses and the ham. Season to taste with nutmeg and salt and pepper. Beat in the cream and eggs to make a thick paste.

2 Bring a large pan of lightly salted water to a boil over medium heat. Add the cannelloni tubes and the olive oil, bring back to a boil, and cook for about 10–12 minutes or until almost tender. Drain and let cool.

3 To make the sauce, melt the butter in a pan over low heat. Stir in the flour and cook, stirring, for 1 minute. Gradually stir in the milk. Add the bay leaves and let simmer, stirring, for 5 minutes. Add the nutmeg and salt and pepper to taste. Remove from the heat and discard the bay leaves.

4 Spoon the filling into a pastry bag and fill the cannelloni.

5 Spoon a little sauce into the bottom of a large ovenproof dish. Place the cannelloni in a single layer in the dish and pour over the remaining sauce. Sprinkle over the grated Parmesan cheese and bake in a preheated oven, 375°F/190°C, for 40–45 minutes. Garnish with sprigs of fresh herb and serve.

S E R V E S   4

8 dried cannelloni tubes
1 tbsp olive oil
1/3 cup freshly grated Parmesan cheese
fresh herb sprigs, to garnish

filling

2 tbsp butter
10 1/2 oz/300 g frozen spinach, thawed and chopped
1/2 cup ricotta cheese
1/3 cup freshly grated Parmesan cheese
1/4 cup chopped ham
pinch of freshly grated nutmeg
2 tbsp heavy cream
2 eggs, beaten lightly
salt and pepper

béchamel sauce

2 tbsp butter
scant 1/4 cup all-purpose flour
1 1/4 cups milk
2 bay leaves
pinch of freshly grated nutmeg

N U T R I T I O N

Calories *520*; Sugars *5 g*; Protein *21 g*; Carbohydrate *23 g*; Fat *39 g*; Saturates *18 g*

⊛⊛⊛   moderate

◔   30 mins

🕑   1 hr 15 mins

🍳 COOK'S TIP

If you prefer, use fresh spinach instead of frozen, but make sure the quantity of fresh spinach is doubled.

This unusual recipe uses chicken and Cumberland sausage, which is then made into individual bite-size cakes.

Tom's Toad-in-the-Hole

SERVES 4 – 6

1 cup all-purpose flour
1 egg, beaten
scant 1 cup milk
5 tbsp water
2 tbsp beef drippings or olive oil
9 oz/250 g chicken breasts
9 oz/250 g Cumberland sausage
salt

to serve
chicken or onion gravy, to serve (optional)
creamy mashed potato

1 Mix the flour and salt together in a bowl, make a well in the center and add the beaten eggs.

2 Add half of the milk and, using a wooden spoon, work in the flour slowly. Beat the mixture until smooth, then add the remaining milk and water. Beat again until the mixture is smooth. Let stand for at least 1 hour.

3 Add the drippings or oil to individual baking pans or to 1 large baking pan. Cut up the chicken and sausage so that you get a generous piece in each individual pan or several sprinkled around the large pan.

4 Heat the pans or pan in a preheated oven, 425°F/220°C, for 5 minutes until very hot. Remove the pans from the oven and pour in the batter, leaving space for the mixture to expand.

5 Return the pans to the oven to cook for about 35 minutes until risen and golden-brown. Do not open the oven door for at least 30 minutes.

6 Serve the toad-in-the-hole while hot with chicken or onion gravy and creamy mashed potato.

NUTRITION
Calories *470*; Sugars *4 g*; Protein *28 g*;
Carbohydrate *30 g*; Fat *27 g*; Saturates *12 g*

easy

1 hr 15 mins

40 mins

 COOK'S TIP

Use skinless, boneless chicken legs instead of chicken breast in the recipe. Instead of Cumberland sausage, use your favorite variety of sausage.

A hot pot is a lamb casserole, made with carrots and onions and with a potato topping. The leg steaks are an interesting alternative.

Hot Pot Chops

1 Using a sharp knife, trim any excess fat from the lamb steaks.

2 Season both sides of the steaks with salt and pepper to taste and arrange them in a single layer on a cookie sheet.

3 Alternate layers of sliced onion, carrot, and potato on top of each lamb steak, ending with a layer of potato.

4 Brush the tops of the potato lightly with oil, season to taste with salt and pepper, then sprinkle with a little dried rosemary.

5 Bake in a preheated oven, 350°F/180°C, for 25–30 minutes or until the lamb is tender and cooked through.

6 Drain the lamb on paper towels and transfer to a warmed serving plate.

7 Garnish with fresh rosemary sprigs and serve accompanied with a selection of steamed green vegetables.

SERVES 4

4 lean, boneless lamb leg steaks,
    about 4½ oz/125 g each
1 small onion, sliced thinly
1 carrot, sliced thinly
1 potato, sliced thinly
1 tsp olive oil
1 tsp dried rosemary
salt and pepper
fresh rosemary sprigs, to garnish
freshly steamed green vegetables, to serve

NUTRITION
Calories *250*; Sugars *2 g*; Protein *27 g*;
Carbohydrate *8 g*; Fat *12 g*; Saturates *5 g*

⭐⭐ easy

🕐 10 mins

🕐 30 mins

🍳 **COOK'S TIP**

This recipe would work well with boneless chicken breasts. Pound the chicken slightly with a meat mallet so the pieces are the same thickness throughout.

A satisfying bake of lean ground beef, zucchini, and tomatoes, cooked in a lowfat "custard" with a cheese crust.

Beef *and* Tomato Gratin

SERVES 4

12 oz/350 g lean ground beef
1 large onion, chopped finely
1 tsp dried mixed herbs
1 tbsp all-purpose flour
1¼ cups beef bouillon
1 tbsp tomato paste
2 large tomatoes, sliced thinly
4 zucchini, sliced thinly
2 tbsp cornstarch
1¼ cups skim milk
¾ cup ricotta cheese
1 egg yolk
scant ¾ cup freshly grated Parmesan cheese
salt and pepper

NUTRITION

Calories *278*; Sugars *10 g*; Protein *29 g*;
Carbohydrate *20 g*; Fat *10 g*; Saturates *4 g*

moderate

10 mins

1 hr 15 mins

1 Dry-cook the beef and onion in a large skillet over low heat, stirring occasionally, for 4–5 minutes until the meat is browned.

2 Stir in the dried mixed herbs, flour, bouillon, and tomato paste, and season to taste with salt and pepper. Bring to a boil, reduce the heat, and let simmer for 30 minutes or until the mixture has thickened.

3 Transfer the beef mixture to an ovenproof gratin dish. Cover with a layer of sliced tomatoes and then add a layer of sliced zucchini.

4 Blend the cornstarch with a little milk to a smooth paste. Pour the rest of the milk into a pan and bring to a boil over low heat. Add the cornstarch mixture and cook, stirring constantly, for 1–2 minutes until thickened. Remove from the heat and beat in the ricotta cheese and egg yolk. Season to taste with salt and pepper.

5 Spread the white sauce over the layer of zucchini. Place the dish on a cookie sheet and sprinkle the grated Parmesan cheese evenly over the top. Bake in a preheated oven, 375°F/190°C, for about 25–30 minutes or until the topping is golden-brown and bubbling. Serve hot.

COOK'S TIP

Replace the ground beef with lamb and the zucchini with eggplant for a quick and easy moussaka.

This slow-cooked beef stew is flavored with oranges, red wine, and porcini mushrooms.

Rich Beef Stew

1 Heat the vegetable oil and butter in a large skillet over low heat. Add the onions and cook, stirring occasionally, for 5 minutes or until golden. Remove the onions with a draining spoon, set aside, and keep warm.

2 Add the beef to the skillet and cook, stirring constantly, for 5 minutes or until browned all over.

3 Return the onions to the skillet and add the bouillon, wine, oregano, and sugar, stirring to mix well. Transfer the mixture to a casserole.

4 Pare the peel from the orange and cut it into strips. Slice the orange flesh into rings. Add the orange rings and the peel to the casserole. Cook in a preheated oven, 350°F/180°C, for 1¼ hours.

5 Meanwhile, soak the porcini mushrooms in 4 tablespoons of warm water for 30 minutes.

6 Peel and halve the tomatoes. Add the tomatoes, porcini mushrooms, and their soaking liquid to the casserole. Cook for another 20 minutes until the beef is tender and the juices thickened. Serve with cooked rice or potatoes.

SERVES 4

1 tbsp vegetable oil
1 tbsp butter
8 oz/225 g pearl onions, halved
1 lb 5 oz/600 g stewing steak, diced into 1½-inch/4-cm chunks
1¼ cups beef bouillon
⅔ cup red wine
4 tbsp chopped fresh oregano
1 tbsp sugar
1 orange
1 oz/25 g dried porcini mushrooms
8 oz/225 g fresh plum tomatoes
freshly cooked rice or potatoes, to serve

NUTRITION
Calories 388; Sugars 15 g; Protein 30 g; Carbohydrate 16 g; Fat 21 g; Saturates 9 g

✪✪✪   moderate
🖐   45 mins
🕐   1 hr 45 mins

🍲 **COOK'S TIP**

If you cannot find dried porcini mushrooms, use sliced fresh mushrooms instead, and omit Step 5.

A different twist is given to this popular, traditional pasta dish with a rich, but wonderfully subtle sauce.

Meatballs *in* Red Wine Sauce

SERVES 4

⅔ cup milk
generous 2½ cups fresh white bread crumbs
2 tbsp butter
9 tbsp olive oil
3 cups sliced oyster mushrooms
¼ cup whole-wheat flour
generous ¾ cup beef bouillon
⅔ cup red wine
4 tomatoes, peeled and chopped
1 tbsp tomato paste
1 tsp brown sugar
1 tbsp finely chopped fresh basil
12 shallots, chopped
4 cups ground steak
1 tsp paprika
1 lb/450 g dried tagliatelle
salt and pepper
fresh basil sprigs, to garnish

NUTRITION
Calories *811*; Sugars *7 g*; Protein *30 g*;
Carbohydrate *76 g*; Fat *43 g*; Saturates *12 g*

✪✪✪   moderate
🕑   45 mins
🕐   1 hr 30 mins

1 Pour the milk into a bowl, add the bread crumbs, and let soak for 30 minutes.

2 Heat half of the butter and 4 tablespoons of the olive oil in a large pan over low heat. Add the mushrooms and cook for 4 minutes. Stir in the flour and cook, stirring, for 2 minutes. Add the bouillon and wine and let simmer for 15 minutes. Add the tomatoes, tomato paste, sugar, and basil. Season to taste with salt and pepper and let simmer for 30 minutes.

3 Mix the shallots, steak, and paprika with the soaked bread crumbs and season to taste with salt and pepper. Shape the mixture into 14 meatballs.

4 Heat 4 tablespoons of the rest of the oil and butter in a large skillet over medium heat. Add the meatballs and cook, turning frequently, until browned all over. Transfer to a deep casserole, pour over the red wine sauce, cover, and bake in a preheated oven, 350°F/180°C, for 30 minutes.

5 Bring a large pan of lightly salted water to a boil over medium heat. Add the tagliatelle and the remaining olive oil, bring back to a boil, and cook for about 8–10 minutes or until tender but still firm to the bite. Drain and transfer to a warmed serving dish. Remove the casserole from the oven and let cool for 3 minutes. Pour the meatballs and sauce onto the pasta, garnish with a few sprigs of fresh basil, and serve.

Any variety of long pasta, such as fettuccine or tagliatelle, could be used for this very tasty dish from Sicily.

Sicilian Spaghetti Cake

1 Brush an 8-inch/20-cm loose-bottom circular cake pan with olive oil and place a disc of oiled baking parchment in the bottom. Cut the eggplants into slanting slices, ¼ inch/5 mm thick. Heat some of the olive oil in a skillet over low heat. Add a few slices of eggplant at a time and cook until lightly browned, turning once, and adding more oil as necessary. Drain on paper towels.

2 Put the ground beef, onion, and garlic into a pan and cook over low heat, stirring frequently, until browned all over. Add the tomato paste, tomatoes, Worcestershire sauce, and herbs. Season to taste with salt and pepper. Let simmer gently for 10 minutes, stirring occasionally, then add the olives and bell pepper and cook for another 10 minutes.

3 Bring a large pan of lightly salted water to a boil over medium heat. Add the spaghetti, bring back to a boil, and cook for 8–10 minutes or until tender, but still firm to the bite. Drain and transfer the spaghetti to a bowl. Mix in the meat mixture and Parmesan cheese, tossing together with 2 forks.

4 Lay overlapping slices of eggplant over the bottom and up the sides of the cake pan. Add the meat mixture and cover with the remaining eggplant.

5 Stand the cake pan in a baking pan and cook in a preheated oven, 400°F/ 200°C, for 40 minutes. Remove from the oven and let stand for 5 minutes, then loosen around the edges and invert onto a warmed serving dish, releasing the pan clip. Remove the baking parchment. Serve immediately.

SERVES 4

⅔ cup olive oil, plus extra for brushing
2 eggplants
generous 3 cups finely ground lean beef
1 onion, chopped
2 garlic cloves, crushed
2 tbsp tomato paste
14 oz/400 g canned chopped tomatoes
1 tsp Worcestershire sauce
1 tsp chopped fresh oregano or marjoram or
    ½ tsp dried oregano or marjoram
½ cup pitted black olives, sliced
1 green, red, or yellow bell pepper, seeded
    and chopped
6 oz/175 g dried spaghetti
generous 1 cup freshly grated Parmesan
    cheese
salt and pepper

NUTRITION
Calories *876*; Sugars *10 g*; Protein *37 g*;
Carbohydrate *39 g*; Fat *65 g*; Saturates *18 g*

★★★   moderate
🕑   30 mins
🕐   1 hr 20 mins

The sauce in this delicious baked pasta dish can be used as an alternative sauce for the classic spaghetti bolognese.

Lasagna Verde

SERVES 6

Ragù Sauce (see page 15)
1 tbsp olive oil
8 oz/225 g fresh or dried lasagna verde
1 tbsp butter, for greasing
2½ cups Béchamel Sauce (see page 73)
⅔ cup freshly grated Parmesan cheese
salt
mixed salad greens, to serve

NUTRITION
Calories 619; Sugars 7 g; Protein 29 g;
Carbohydrate 21 g; Fat 45 g; Saturates 19 g

✪✪✪✪ challenging
🕐 1 hr 45 mins
🕐 1 hr

1 Make the Ragù Sauce, but cook for 10–12 minutes longer than the time given, in an uncovered pan, to allow the excess liquid to evaporate. It needs to be reduced to a thick paste.

2 Have ready a large pan of lightly salted boiling water and add the olive oil. Drop the lasagna sheets into the boiling water, a few at a time, and bring back to a boil before adding further lasagna sheets. If you are using fresh lasagna, cook the sheets for a total of 8 minutes. If you are using dried or partly precooked pasta, cook it according to the instructions given on the package.

3 Remove the lasagna sheets from the pan with a draining spoon or tongs. Spread them out in a single layer on damp dish cloths until required.

4 Grease a rectangular ovenproof dish, about 10–11 inches/25–28 cm long, with the butter. To assemble the dish, spoon a little of the meat sauce into the prepared dish and cover with a layer of lasagna, then spoon over a little béchamel sauce and sprinkle with some of the Parmesan cheese. Continue making layers in this way, covering the final layer of lasagna sheets with the remaining béchamel sauce.

5 Sprinkle the remaining grated Parmesan cheese over the top and bake in a preheated oven, 375°F/190°C, for about 40 minutes or until the sauce is golden-brown and bubbling. Serve with salad greens.

A recipe that has both Italian and Greek origins, this dish may be served hot or cold, cut into thick, satisfying squares.

Pasticcio

1 To make the sauce, heat the olive oil in a large skillet over medium heat. Add the onion and red bell pepper and cook for 3 minutes. Stir in the garlic and cook for another minute. Stir in the beef and cook, stirring frequently, until it is no longer pink.

2 Add the chopped tomatoes and wine, stir well, and bring to a boil. Let simmer, uncovered, for 20 minutes or until the sauce is fairly thick. Stir in the parsley and anchovies and season to taste with salt and pepper.

3 Bring a large pan of lightly salted water to a boil over medium heat. Add the fusilli and olive oil, bring back to a boil, and cook for 8–10 minutes or until tender but still firm to the bite. Drain, then transfer the fusilli to a bowl. Stir in the cream and set aside.

4 To make the topping, beat the yogurt, eggs, and nutmeg together. Season to taste with salt and pepper.

5 Brush a shallow ovenproof dish with olive oil. Spoon in half of the fusilli and cover with half of the meat sauce. Repeat these layers, then spread the topping evenly over the final layer. Sprinkle the Parmesan cheese on top.

6 Bake in a preheated oven, 375°F/190°C, for 25 minutes or until the topping is golden-brown and bubbling. Garnish with a few sprigs of fresh rosemary and serve hot.

SERVES 6

8 oz/225 g dried fusilli, or other pasta shapes
1 tbsp olive oil
4 tbsp heavy cream
salt
fresh rosemary sprigs, to garnish

sauce

2 tbsp olive oil, plus extra for brushing
1 onion, sliced thinly
1 red bell pepper, seeded and chopped
2 garlic cloves, chopped
1 lb 6 oz/625 g lean ground beef
14 oz/400 g canned chopped tomatoes
1/2 cup dry white wine
2 tbsp chopped fresh parsley
1 3/4 oz/50 g canned anchovies, drained and chopped
salt and pepper

topping

1 1/4 cups plain yogurt
3 eggs
pinch of freshly grated nutmeg
1/2 cup freshly grated Parmesan cheese

NUTRITION

Calories *590*; Sugars *8 g*; Protein *34 g*; Carbohydrate *23 g*; Fat *39 g*; Saturates *16 g*

⭐⭐⭐   moderate

🕑   35 mins

🕐   1 hr 15 mins

Vegan *and* Vegetarian

Anyone who ever thought that vegetarian meals were dull will be proved wrong by the rich variety of dishes in this chapter. You'll recognize influences from Middle Eastern and Italian cooking, such as the Pasta and Bean Casserole, Roman Focaccia, and Sun-Dried Tomato Loaf, but there are also traditional recipes such as Baked Cheesecake and Fruit Crumble. They all make exciting treats at any time of year and for virtually any occasion. Don't be afraid to substitute some of your own personal favorite ingredients wherever appropriate.

Thick pasta tubes are filled with a mixture of seasoned, chopped mushrooms, and baked in a rich tomato sauce.

Mushroom Cannelloni

SERVES 4

12 oz/350 g crimini mushrooms, chopped finely
1 onion, chopped finely
1 garlic clove, minced
1 tbsp chopped fresh thyme
½ tsp ground nutmeg
4 tbsp dry white wine
scant 1 cup fresh white bread crumbs
12 dried quick-cook cannelloni
salt and pepper
shavings of Parmesan cheese, to garnish (optional)

tomato sauce

1 large red bell pepper
¾ cup dry white wine
scant 2 cups strained tomatoes
2 tbsp tomato paste
2 bay leaves
1 tsp superfine sugar

NUTRITION
Calories *156*; Sugars *8 g*; Protein *6 g*;
Carbohydrate *21 g*; Fat *1 g*; Saturates *0.2 g*

⭐⭐⭐⭐ challenging

🕐 35 mins

🕐 1 hr 30 mins

1 Place the mushrooms, onion, and garlic in a large pan. Stir in the thyme, nutmeg, and the wine. Bring to a boil over low heat, cover, and let simmer for 10 minutes. Stir in the bread crumbs to bind the mixture together and season to taste with salt and pepper. Remove the pan from the heat and let cool for 10 minutes.

2 To make the sauce, halve and seed the bell pepper, place on the broiler rack, and cook under a preheated hot broiler for 8–10 minutes until charred. Let cool for 10 minutes.

3 Once the bell pepper has cooled, peel off the skin. Chop the flesh and place in a food processor with the wine. Blend until smooth, then pour into a pan. Mix the remaining sauce ingredients with the bell pepper and wine. Bring to a boil and let simmer for 10 minutes. Remove and discard the bay leaves.

4 Cover the bottom of an ovenproof dish with a thin layer of the sauce. Fill the cannelloni with the mushroom mixture and place in a single layer in the dish. Spoon over the remaining sauce, then cover with foil, and bake in a preheated oven, 400°F/200°C for 35–40 minutes. Garnish with Parmesan cheese, if desired, and serve hot.

🍳 **COOK'S TIP**

Crimini mushrooms, also known as champignons de Paris, are common cultivated mushrooms that may have brown or white caps.

A satisfying winter dish, this is a slow-cooked, one-pot meal. The navy beans need to be soaked overnight, so prepare well in advance.

Pasta *and* Bean Casserole

1 Put the beans into a large pan, cover them with water, and bring to a boil over high heat. Boil the beans rapidly for 20 minutes, then drain and set aside until required.

2 Bring a large pan of lightly salted water to a boil over medium heat. Add the penne and 1 tablespoon of the olive oil, bring back to a boil and cook for 3 minutes. Drain and set aside.

3 Place the beans in a large ovenproof casserole, pour on the vegetable bouillon, and stir in the remaining olive oil, the onions, garlic, bay leaves, herbs, wine, and tomato paste.

4 Bring to a boil over medium heat, cover the casserole, and cook in a preheated oven, 350°F/180°C, for 2 hours.

5 Remove the casserole from the oven and add the reserved pasta, the celery, fennel, mushrooms, and tomatoes, and season to taste with salt and pepper.

6 Stir in the sugar and sprinkle on the bread crumbs. Cover the casserole, return to the oven, and continue cooking for another hour. Serve hot with salad greens.

SERVES 4

generous 1 cup dried navy beans, soaked overnight and drained
8 oz/225 g dried penne, or other short pasta shapes
6 tbsp olive oil
3½ cups vegetable bouillon
2 large onions, sliced
2 garlic cloves, chopped
2 bay leaves
1 tsp dried oregano
1 tsp dried thyme
5 tbsp red wine
2 tbsp tomato paste
2 celery stalks, sliced
1 fennel bulb, sliced
scant 2 cups sliced mushrooms
8 oz/225 g tomatoes, sliced
1 tsp dark muscovado sugar
scant 1 cup dry white bread crumbs
salt and pepper
salad greens, to serve

NUTRITION
Calories *323*; Sugars *5 g*; Protein *13 g*;
Carbohydrate *41 g*; Fat *12 g*; Saturates *2 g*

✪✪✪   moderate
🕑   25 mins
🕐   3 hrs 30 mins

This savory tart combines lentils and red bell peppers in a tasty whole-wheat shell. This tart is suitable for vegans.

Lentil *and* Red Bell Pepper Tart

SERVES 6

pie dough

1¾ cups plain whole-wheat flour, plus extra for dusting
⅓ cup vegan margarine, cut into small pieces
4 tbsp water

filling

¾ cup split red lentils, rinsed
1¼ cups vegetable bouillon
1 tbsp vegan margarine
1 onion, chopped
2 red bell peppers, seeded and diced
1 tsp yeast extract
1 tbsp tomato paste
3 tbsp chopped fresh parsley
pepper

NUTRITION
Calories 374; Sugars 5 g; Protein 13 g; Carbohydrate 44 g; Fat 17 g; Saturates 7 g

easy

15–20 mins

50 mins

1 To make the pie dough, sift the flour into a large bowl and add any bran remaining in the strainer. Add the vegan margarine and rub it in with your fingertips until the mixture resembles fine bread crumbs. Stir in the water and mix to form a dough. Wrap in plastic wrap and let chill in the refrigerator for 30 minutes.

2 Meanwhile, make the filling. Put the lentils in a pan with the bouillon, bring to a boil over medium heat, then let simmer for 10 minutes until the lentils are tender and can be mashed to a paste.

3 Melt the margarine in a small pan over low heat. Add the onion and red bell peppers, and cook, stirring occasionally, until just softened. Add the lentil paste, yeast extract, tomato paste, and chopped parsley. Season to taste with pepper. Mix well.

4 Roll out the dough on a lightly floured counter, and use to line a 9½-inch/ 24-cm loose-bottom tart pan. Prick the bottom of the pie dough with a fork and spoon the lentil mixture into the pie shell.

5 Bake in a preheated oven, 400°F/200°C, for 30 minutes until the filling is firm. Serve hot.

COOK'S TIP

Add some corn kernels to the flan at step 4 for a colorful and tasty change, if you prefer.

A hearty casserole of black-eye peas in a rich, sweet tomato sauce flavored with molasses and mustard.

Spicy Black-Eye Peas

1 Rinse the peas and place in a pan. Cover with water, bring to a boil over high heat, and boil rapidly for 10 minutes. Drain and place in a casserole.

2 Meanwhile, heat the vegetable oil in a skillet over low heat. Add the onions and cook, stirring occasionally, for 5 minutes. Stir in the honey, molasses, soy sauce, mustard, and tomato paste. Pour in the bouillon, bring to a boil, and pour over the peas.

3 Tie the bay leaf and herbs together with a piece of string and add to the casserole. Using a vegetable peeler, pare off 3 pieces of orange peel and mix into the peas, along with plenty of pepper. Cover and cook in a preheated oven, 300°F/150°C, for 1 hour.

4 Extract the juice from the orange and blend with the cornstarch to form a smooth paste. Remove the casserole from the oven and stir the cornstarch paste into the peas along with the red bell peppers. Cover, return to the oven, and cook for another hour, until the sauce is rich and thick and the peas are tender. Discard the herbs and orange peel.

5 Garnish the casserole with fresh parsley and serve with crusty bread.

SERVES 4

2 cups black-eye peas, soaked overnight in cold water
1 tbsp vegetable oil
2 onions, chopped
1 tbsp honey
2 tbsp molasses
4 tbsp dark soy sauce
1 tsp dry mustard powder
4 tbsp tomato paste
scant 2 cups vegetable bouillon
1 bay leaf
1 fresh rosemary sprig, thyme sprig, and sage sprig
1 small orange
1 tbsp cornstarch
2 red bell peppers, seeded and diced pepper
2 tbsp chopped fresh Italian parsley, to garnish
crusty bread, to serve

NUTRITION

Calories *233*; Sugars *21 g*; Protein *11 g*; Carbohydrate *42 g*; Fat *4 g*; Saturates *1 g*

✪✪✪   moderate

🕐   15 mins

🕐   1 hr 30 mins

This freshly made bread is an ideal accompaniment to salads and soups and is suitable for vegans.

Garlic *and* Sage Bread

SERVES 6

1 tbsp vegan margarine, for greasing
2¼ cups brown bread flour, plus extra for dusting
1 sachet active dry yeast
3 tbsp chopped fresh sage
2 tsp sea salt
3 cloves garlic, chopped finely
1 tsp honey
⅔ cup lukewarm water

1 Grease a cookie sheet with vegan margarine. Sift the flour into a large bowl and stir in the bran remaining in the strainer.

2 Stir in the dry yeast, sage, and half of the sea salt. Set aside 1 teaspoon of the chopped garlic for sprinkling and stir the rest into the bowl. Add the honey with the lukewarm water and mix to form a dough.

3 Knead the dough on a lightly floured counter for 5 minutes. Alternatively, use an electric mixer with a dough hook.

4 Place the dough in a greased bowl, cover, and let rise in a warm place until doubled in size.

5 Knead the dough again for a few minutes, shape it into a circle (see Cook's Tip), and place on the cookie sheet.

6 Cover and let rise for another 30 minutes or until springy to the touch. Sprinkle with the rest of the sea salt and garlic.

7 Bake the loaf in a preheated oven, 400°F/200°C, for 25–30 minutes. Transfer the loaf to a wire rack to cool completely before serving.

NUTRITION
Calories *207*; Sugars *3 g*; Protein *9 g*; Carbohydrate *42 g*; Fat *2 g*; Saturates *0 g*

★★★   moderate

🕐   1 hr 15 mins

🕐   30 mins

 COOK'S TIP
Roll the dough into a long sausage and then curve it into a circular shape.

Roman focaccia makes a delicious snack on its own or served with a selection of vegetarian cheeses and salad for a quick supper.

Roman Focaccia

1 Place the yeast and the sugar in a small bowl and mix with ½ cup of the water. Let the mixture ferment in a warm place for 15 minutes.

2 Sift the flour and the salt into a large bowl. Add the yeast mixture, half of the rosemary, and the remaining water, and mix to form a smooth dough. Knead the dough for 4 minutes, then cover the dough with oiled plastic wrap and let rise for 30 minutes or until doubled in size.

3 Meanwhile, heat the olive oil in a large pan over low heat. Add the onions and garlic and cook, stirring occasionally, for 5 minutes or until softened. Cover the pan and continue to cook for 7–8 minutes or until the onions are lightly caramelized.

4 Remove the dough from the bowl and knead it on a lightly floured counter, then roll out to a square. The dough should be no more than ¼ inch/5 mm thick because it will rise during cooking. Place the dough on a large cookie sheet, pushing out the edges until even.

5 Spread the onions over the dough, and sprinkle with the rest of the rosemary.

6 Bake in a preheated oven, 400°F/200°C, for 25–30 minutes or until golden-brown. Remove from the oven and let cool slightly. Cut the focaccia into 16 squares, garnish with a few fresh rosemary leaves and serve.

MAKES 16 SQUARES

¼ oz/10 g dried yeast
1 tsp granulated sugar
1¼ cups lukewarm water
1 lb/450 g white bread flour, plus extra for dusting
2 tsp salt
3 tbsp chopped fresh rosemary
2 tbsp olive oil
1 lb/450 g mixed red and white onions, sliced into rings
4 garlic cloves, sliced
fresh rosemary leaves, to garnish

NUTRITION
Calories 119; Sugars 2 g; Protein 3 g; Carbohydrate 24 g; Fat 2 g; Saturates 0.3 g

moderate

1 hr

45 mins

This delicious tomato bread is great with cheese or soup or for making an unusual sandwich. This recipe makes one loaf.

Sun-Dried Tomato Loaf

MAKES 1 LOAF

¼ oz/10 g dried yeast
1 tsp granulated sugar
1¼ cups lukewarm water
1 lb/450 g white bread flour, plus extra
    for dusting
1 tsp salt
2 tsp dried basil
2 tbsp sun-dried tomato paste or
    tomato paste
1 tbsp olive oil, for oiling
1 tbsp vegan margarine, for greasing
12 sun-dried tomatoes in oil, drained and cut
    into strips

NUTRITION
Calories 403; Sugars 5 g; Protein 12 g;
Carbohydrate 91 g; Fat 2 g; Saturates 0.3 g

⭐⭐⭐   moderate
🕐   1 hr 45 mins
🕐   35 mins

1 Place the yeast and sugar in a bowl and mix with ½ cup of the water. Let the mixture ferment in a warm place for 15 minutes.

2 Sift the flour and salt into a bowl. Make a well in the center and add the basil, yeast mixture, tomato paste, and half of the remaining water. Using a wooden spoon, draw the flour into the liquid and mix to form a dough, adding the rest of the water gradually.

3 Knead the dough on a floured counter for 5 minutes. Cover with oiled plastic wrap and let stand in a warm place for 30 minutes or until doubled in size.

4 Lightly grease a 2-lb/900-g loaf pan with vegan margarine.

5 Remove the dough from the bowl and knead in the sun-dried tomatoes. Knead again for 2–3 minutes.

6 Place the dough in the prepared pan and let rise for 30–40 minutes or until it has doubled in size again. Bake in a preheated oven, 375°F/190°C, for about 30–35 minutes or until golden and the bottom sounds hollow when tapped. Let cool on a wire rack.

 COOK'S TIP

You could make mini sun-dried tomato loaves for children. Divide the dough into 8 equal portions, let rise, and bake in mini-loaf pans for 20 minutes.

Bell peppers become wonderfully sweet and mild when they are roasted in the oven, and make this bread delicious.

Roasted Bell Pepper Bread

1 Grease a 9-inch/23-cm deep circular cake pan with vegan margarine.

2 Place the bell peppers and rosemary in a shallow roasting pan. Pour over the olive oil and roast in a preheated oven, 400°F/200°C, for 20 minutes or until charred. Remove the skin from the bell peppers and cut the flesh into slices.

3 Place the yeast and sugar in a small bowl and mix with ½ cup of lukewarm water. Let the mixture ferment in a warm place for 15 minutes.

4 Sift the flour and salt into a large bowl. Stir in the yeast mixture and the remaining water and mix to form a smooth dough.

5 Knead the dough on a floured counter for about 5 minutes. Cover with oiled plastic wrap and let rise for 30 minutes or until doubled in size.

6 Cut the dough into 3 equal portions. Roll the portions into circles slightly larger than the cake pan. Place 1 circle in the bottom of the pan so that it reaches up the sides of the pan by about ¾ inch/2 cm. Top with half of the bell pepper mixture.

7 Place the second circle of dough on top, followed by the remaining bell pepper mixture. Place the last circle of dough on top, pushing the edges of the dough down the sides of the pan.

8 Cover the dough with oiled plastic wrap and let rise for 30–40 minutes. Bake in the preheated oven for 45 minutes until golden or the bottom sounds hollow when lightly tapped. Let cool on a wire rack and serve warm.

SERVES 4

1 tbsp vegan margarine, for greasing
1 red bell pepper, halved and seeded
1 yellow bell pepper, halved and seeded
2 fresh rosemary sprigs
1 tbsp olive oil
¼ oz/10 g dried yeast
1 tsp granulated sugar
1¼ cups lukewarm water
1 lb/450 g white bread flour, plus extra for dusting
1 tsp salt
1 tbsp olive oil, for oiling

NUTRITION
Calories 426; Sugars 4 g; Protein 12 g; Carbohydrate 90 g; Fat 4 g; Saturates 1 g

★★★ moderate
🖐 1 hr 45 mins
🕐 1 hr 5 mins

These vegan slices are ideal for children's lunches. They are full of flavor and made with healthy ingredients.

Apricot Slices

MAKES 12 BARS

pie dough

⅓ cup vegan margarine, cut into small pieces, plus extra for greasing

1¾ cups whole-wheat flour, plus extra for dusting

½ cup finely ground mixed nuts

4 tbsp water

1–2 tsp soy milk, for glazing

filling

1 cup dried apricots

grated peel of 1 orange

1¼ cups apple juice

1 tsp ground cinnamon

⅓ cup raisins

NUTRITION

Calories *198*; Sugars *13 g*; Protein *4 g*; Carbohydrate *25 g*; Fat *9 g*; Saturates *2 g*

⭐⭐⭐ moderate

🍳 50 mins

🕐 1 hr

1 Lightly grease a 9-inch/23-cm square cake pan with vegan margarine. To make the pie dough, place the flour and nuts in a large bowl. Add the margarine and rub it in with your fingertips until the mixture resembles bread crumbs. Stir in the water and mix to form a dough. Wrap in plastic wrap and let chill in the refrigerator for 30 minutes.

2 To make the filling, place the apricots, orange peel, and apple juice in a small pan and bring to a boil over low heat. Let simmer for 30 minutes until the apricots are mushy. Let cool slightly, then process in a food processor or blender to a paste. Alternatively, press the mixture through a fine strainer. Stir in the cinnamon and raisins.

3 Divide the pie dough in half, roll out one half on a lightly floured counter and use to line the bottom of the prepared pan. Spread the apricot paste over the top and brush the edges with water. Roll out the rest of the dough to fit over the top of the apricot paste. Press down and seal the edges.

4 Prick the top of the pie dough with a fork and brush with soy milk. Bake in a preheated oven, 400°F/200°C, for 20–25 minutes until the pastry is golden. Let cool slightly before cutting into 12 bars. Serve either warm or cold.

👑 **COOK'S TIP**

These slices will keep in an airtight container for 3–4 days.

This cheesecake has a rich creamy texture, but contains no dairy produce at all, because it is made with bean curd.

Baked Cheesecake

1 Grease a 7-inch/18-cm circular loose-bottom cake pan with vegan margarine.

2 Mix the graham cracker crumbs and melted margarine together in a bowl. Press the mixture into the bottom of the prepared pan.

3 Put the chopped dates, lemon juice, lemon peel, and water into a saucepan and bring to a boil over low heat. Let simmer for 5 minutes until the dates are soft, then mash them coarsely with a fork.

4 Place the mixture in a blender or food processor with the bean curd, apple juice, mashed banana, and vanilla extract and process until the mixture forms a thick, smooth paste.

5 Pour the bean curd paste onto the prepared cracker crumb base and gently smooth the surface with the back of a spoon.

6 Bake in a preheated oven, 350°F/180°C, for 30–40 minutes, until lightly golden. Let cool in the pan, then let chill in the refrigerator before serving.

7 Place the chopped mango in a blender and process until smooth. Serve it as a sauce with the cheesecake.

SERVES 6

4 tbsp vegan margarine, melted, plus extra
  for greasing
2¼ cups graham cracker crumbs
⅓ cup chopped pitted dates
4 tbsp lemon juice
grated peel of 1 lemon
3 tbsp water
12 oz/350 g firm bean curd (drained weight)
⅔ cup apple juice
1 banana, mashed
1 tsp vanilla extract
1 mango, peeled, pitted, and chopped

NUTRITION
Calories 282; Sugars 17 g; Protein 9 g;
Carbohydrate 29 g; Fat 15 g; Saturates 4 g

✪✪✪   moderate
             2 hrs 15 mins
             45 mins

🍳 COOK'S TIP

Silken bean curd may be substituted for the firm bean curd to give a softer texture. It will take 40–50 minutes to set.

Any fruits in season can be used in this wholesome dessert. It is suitable for vegans as it contains no dairy produce.

Fruit Crumble

SERVES 6

1 tbsp vegan margarine, for greasing
6 dessert pears, peeled, cored, cut into fourths, and sliced
1 tbsp chopped preserved ginger
1 tbsp molasses
2 tbsp orange juice

topping
1½ cups all-purpose flour
6 tbsp vegan margarine, cut into small pieces
¼ cup slivered almonds
⅓ cup porridge oats
1¾ oz/50 g molasses
soy custard, to serve

1 Lightly grease a 4-cup/1-liter ovenproof dish with vegan margarine.

2 Mix the pears, ginger, molasses, and orange juice together in a bowl. Spoon the mixture into the prepared dish.

3 To make the crumble topping, sift the flour into a large bowl. Add the margarine and rub it in with your fingertips until the mixture resembles fine bread crumbs. Stir in the slivered almonds, porridge oats, and molasses. Mix well.

4 Sprinkle the crumble topping evenly over the pear and ginger mixture.

5 Bake in a preheated oven, 375°F/190°C, for 30 minutes or until the topping is golden and the fruit tender. Serve hot with soy custard, if using.

NUTRITION
Calories *426*; Sugars *37 g*; Protein *8 g*; Carbohydrate *67 g*; Fat *16 g*; Saturates *4 g*

easy
10 mins
30 mins

🍳 COOK'S TIP

Stir 1 teaspoon ground allspice into the crumble mixture at Step 3 for added flavor, if you prefer.

This is a healthy, but still absolutely delicious variation of the classic sponge layer cake and is suitable for vegans.

Eggless Sponge

1 Lightly grease 2 x 8-inch/20-cm layer pans with vegan margarine and line with baking parchment.

2 Sift the flour and baking powder into a large bowl, stirring in any bran remaining in the strainer. Stir in the superfine sugar.

3 Pour in the corn oil, water, and vanilla extract. Mix well for about 1 minute or until the mixture is smooth, then divide among the prepared pans.

4 Bake in a preheated oven, 350°F/180°C, for about 25–30 minutes or until the center of the cakes springs back when lightly touched.

5 Let the sponge cakes cool slightly in the pans before turning out and transferring to a wire rack to cool completely.

6 To serve, remove the baking parchment and place one of the sponge cakes on a large serving plate. Cover with the spread and place the other sponge cake on top. Dust the cake with a little superfine sugar before serving.

SERVES 8

2 tbsp vegan margarine, for greasing
1¾ cups whole-wheat self-rising flour
2 tsp baking powder
¾ cup superfine sugar
6 tbsp corn oil
1 cup water
1 tsp vanilla extract
4 tbsp strawberry or raspberry reduced-sugar spread
superfine sugar, for dusting

NUTRITION
Calories *273*; Sugars *27 g*; Protein *3 g*;
Carbohydrate *49 g*; Fat *9 g*; Saturates *1 g*

⭐⭐   easy
🕐   1 hr 15 mins
🕐   30 mins

👨‍🍳 **COOK'S TIP**

To make a citrus-flavored sponge, add the grated zest of ½ lemon or orange to the flour at Step 2. To make a coffee-flavored sponge, replace 2 teaspoons of the flour with instant coffee powder.

Desserts

Confirmed dessert lovers feel a meal is lacking if there isn't a tempting dessert to finish off the menu. Yet it is often possible to combine indulgence with healthy ingredients. A lot of the recipes in this chapter contain fruit, which is the perfect ingredient for healthy desserts that are still deliciously tempting, such as Blackberry Pudding, Raspberry Shortcake, One Roll Fruit Pie, Apple Tart Tatin, and Baked Bananas. Some desserts are also packed full of protein-rich nuts, such as Apricot and Cranberry Tart and Almond Cheesecakes.

This is a slightly different version of an old favorite made with the addition of orange peel and marmalade to give a delicious orange flavor.

Queen *of* Puddings

SERVES 8

2 tbsp butter, plus extra for greasing
2½ cups milk
1¼ cups superfine sugar
finely grated peel of 1 orange
4 eggs, separated
1⅔ cups fresh bread crumbs
6 tbsp orange marmalade
salt

1 Grease a 6-cup/1.5-liter ovenproof dish with a little butter.

2 To make the custard, heat the milk in a pan with the butter, ¼ cup of the superfine sugar, and the orange peel over low heat, until just warm.

3 Whisk the egg yolks in a bowl. Gradually pour the warm milk over the eggs, stirring constantly.

4 Stir the bread crumbs into the pan, then transfer the mixture to the prepared dish and let stand for about 15 minutes.

5 Bake in a preheated oven, 350°F/180°C, for 20–25 minutes or until the custard has just set. Remove from the oven but do not turn the oven off.

6 To make the meringue, whisk the egg whites with a pinch of salt until they stand in soft peaks. Whisk in the remaining sugar, a little at a time.

7 Spread the orange marmalade over the cooked custard, then top with the meringue, spreading it to the edges of the dish.

8 Return to the preheated oven and bake for another 20 minutes until the meringue is crisp and golden.

NUTRITION
Calories *289*; Sugars *46 g*; Protein *6 g*;
Carbohydrate *50 g*; Fat *8 g*; Saturates *4 g*

moderate

25 mins

45 mins

COOK'S TIP

If you prefer a crisper meringue, bake the dessert in the oven for an extra 5 minutes.

Everyone has their own favorite recipe for this dish. This one has added marmalade and grated apples for a really rich and unique taste.

Bread *and* Butter Pudding

1 Use the butter to grease an ovenproof dish and to spread on the slices of bread, then spread the bread with the marmalade.

2 Place a layer of bread in the bottom of the dish and sprinkle with the lemon peel, half of the golden raisins, half of the candied peel, half of the cinnamon, all of the apple, and half of the brown sugar.

3 Add another layer of bread, cutting the slices so they fit in the dish.

4 Sprinkle over most of the remaining golden raisins and all the remaining candied peel, cinnamon, and brown sugar, sprinkling it evenly over the bread. Top with a final layer of bread, again cutting to fit the dish.

5 Lightly beat the eggs and milk together and strain the mixture over the bread in the dish. If time allows, let the dessert stand for 20–30 minutes.

6 Sprinkle the top with the raw brown sugar and sprinkle over the remaining golden raisins. Cook in a preheated oven, 400°F/200°C, for 50–60 minutes, until risen and golden-brown. Serve immediately or let cool and serve cold.

S E R V E S 6

5 tbsp butter, softened
4–5 slices white or brown bread
4 tbsp chunky orange marmalade
grated peel of 1 lemon
½–¾ cup golden raisins
¼ cup chopped candied peel
1 tsp ground cinnamon or allspice
1 cooking apple, peeled, cored, and coarsely grated
scant ½ cup brown sugar
3 eggs
generous 2 cups milk
2 tbsp raw brown sugar

N U T R I T I O N
Calories 427; Sugars 63 g; Protein 9 g; Carbohydrate 74 g; Fat 13 g; Saturates 7 g

⭐⭐⭐   moderate
🕐   45 mins
🕐   1 hr

This is a favorite dessert, which can easily be adapted to suit all types of fruit if plums are not available.

Plum Cobbler

SERVES 6

1 tbsp butter, for greasing
2 lb 4 oz/1 kg plums, pitted and sliced
½ cup superfine sugar
1 tbsp lemon juice
2¼ cups all-purpose flour
2 tsp baking powder
⅓ cup granulated sugar
1 egg, beaten
⅔ cup buttermilk
6 tbsp butter, melted and cooled
heavy cream, to serve (optional)

1 Lightly grease an 8-cup/2-liter ovenproof dish with a little butter.

2 Mix the plums, superfine sugar, lemon juice, and ¼ cup of the all-purpose flour together in a bowl.

3 Spoon the coated plums into the bottom of the prepared dish, spreading them out evenly.

4 Sift the remaining flour and baking powder into a bowl. Add the granulated sugar and stir well.

5 Add the beaten egg, buttermilk, and cooled melted butter. Mix gently to form a soft dough.

6 Place spoonfuls of the dough on top of the fruit mixture until it is almost completely covered.

7 Bake in a preheated oven, 375°F/190°C, for about 35–40 minutes or until golden-brown and bubbling.

8 Serve the dessert piping hot, with heavy cream, if desired.

NUTRITION
Calories *430*; Sugars *46 g*; Protein *7 g*;
Carbohydrate *79 g*; Fat *12 g*; Saturates *7 g*

★★★ moderate
🕐 10 mins
🕐 40 mins

🍳 **COOK'S TIP**

If you cannot find buttermilk, try using sour cream.

A delicious dessert to make when blackberries are in abundance! If blackberries are unavailable, try using currants or gooseberries.

Blackberry Pudding

1 Lightly grease a large 3½-cup/900-ml ovenproof dish with the butter.

2 Gently mix the blackberries and superfine sugar together in a large bowl until the blackberries are well coated in the sugar.

3 Transfer the blackberry and sugar mixture to the prepared dish.

4 Beat the egg and brown sugar in a separate bowl. Stir in the melted butter and milk.

5 Sift the flour into the egg and butter mixture and fold together lightly with a figure-eight movement to form a smooth batter.

6 Carefully spread the batter over the blackberry and sugar mixture.

7 Bake the dessert in a preheated oven, 350°F/180°C, for about 25–30 minutes or until the topping is firm and golden.

8 Sprinkle the dessert with a little sugar and serve hot.

SERVES 4

1 tbsp butter, for greasing
1 lb/450 g blackberries
⅓ cup superfine sugar, plus extra for sprinkling
1 egg
⅓ cup brown sugar
6 tbsp butter, melted
½ cup milk
scant 1 cup self-rising flour

NUTRITION
Calories *455*; Sugars *47 g*; Protein *7 g*; Carbohydrate *70 g*; Fat *18 g*; Saturates *11 g*

⭐⭐ easy

🕒 15–20 mins

🕐 30 mins

🍳 **COOK'S TIP**

You can add 2 tablespoons of unsweetened cocoa to the batter at Step 5, if you prefer a chocolate flavor.

For this lovely summery dessert, two crisp circles of shortbread are sandwiched together with fresh raspberries and lightly whipped cream.

Raspberry Shortcake

SERVES 8

⅓ cup butter, diced, plus extra for greasing
1½ cups self-rising flour, plus extra for dusting
⅓ cup superfine sugar
1 egg yolk
1 tbsp rose water
2½ cups heavy cream, whipped lightly
1⅓ cups raspberries, plus extra for decoration
confectioners' sugar, for dusting

1 Lightly grease 2 cookie sheets with a little butter.

2 To make the shortcake, sift the flour into a large bowl. Add the butter and rub it in with your fingertips until the mixture resembles bread crumbs.

3 Stir the sugar, egg yolk, and rose water into the mixture and bring together with your fingers to form a soft dough. Divide the dough in half.

4 Roll out each piece of dough on a lightly floured surface into an 8-inch/20-cm circle. Carefully lift each one with the rolling pin onto a prepared cookie sheet. Crimp the edges of the dough.

5 Bake in a preheated oven, 375°F/190°C, for 15 minutes or until lightly golden. Transfer the shortcakes to a wire rack and let cool.

6 Mix the cream and the raspberries together, then spoon on top of one of the shortcakes, spreading it out evenly. Top with the other shortcake circle, dust with a little confectioners' sugar, and decorate with the extra raspberries.

NUTRITION
Calories *496*; Sugars *14 g*; Protein *4 g*; Carbohydrate *30 g*; Fat *41 g*; Saturates *26 g*

easy

40 mins

15 mins

🍲 **COOK'S TIP**

The shortcake can be made a few days in advance and stored in an airtight container until required.

This delicious dessert originated in Australia. Serve it with sharp fruits, such as summer berries, to balance the sweetness of the meringue.

Pavlova

1 Line a cookie sheet with a sheet of baking parchment.

2 Whisk the egg whites with a pinch of salt in a large bowl until they form soft peaks.

3 Whisk in the sugar, a little at a time, whisking well after each addition until all the sugar has been incorporated and the meringue is smooth and glossy.

4 Spoon three-quarters of the meringue onto the prepared cookie sheet, forming a circle 8 inches/20 cm in diameter.

5 Place spoonfuls of the remaining meringue all around the edge of the circle to make a nest shape.

6 Bake in a preheated oven, 275°F/140°C, for 1¼ hours.

7 Turn the heat off, but leave the pavlova in the oven until it is completely cold.

8 To serve, place the pavlova on a serving dish. Spread with the whipped cream, then arrange the fresh fruit on top. Do not decorate the pavlova too far in advance or it will go soggy.

SERVES 6

3 egg whites
¾ cup superfine sugar
1¼ cups heavy cream, whipped lightly
fresh fruit of your choice (raspberries, strawberries, peaches, passion fruit, ground cherries)
salt

NUTRITION
Calories 354; Sugars 34 g; Protein 3 g;
Carbohydrate 34 g; Fat 24 g; Saturates 15 g

✪✪✪   moderate
🍴   1 hr 10 mins
🕐   1 hr 15 mins

👨‍🍳 COOK'S TIP

If you are worried about creating the right shape, draw a circle on the baking parchment, turn the paper over, then spoon the meringue inside the outline.

This is an easy way to make a pie—once you have rolled out the pie dough and filled it with fruit, you just turn the edges in.

One Roll Fruit Pie

SERVES 8

pie dough

⅓ cup butter, cut into small pieces, plus extra for greasing
1½ cups all-purpose flour, plus extra for dusting
1 tbsp water
1 egg, separated
sugar lumps, crushed, for sprinkling

filling

1 lb 5 oz/600 g prepared fruit (rhubarb, gooseberries, plums, damsons)
⅓ cup brown sugar
1 tbsp ground ginger

1 Grease a large cookie sheet with a little butter.

2 To make the pie dough, sift the flour into a large bowl. Add the butter and rub it in with your fingertips until the mixture resembles bread crumbs. Add the water and mix to form a soft dough. Wrap in plastic wrap and let chill in the refrigerator for 30 minutes.

3 Roll out the chilled dough in a lightly floured surface to a circle 14 inches/ 35 cm in diameter.

4 Transfer the dough circle to the center of the prepared cookie sheet. Brush the dough with the egg yolk.

5 To make the filling, mix the prepared fruit with the brown sugar and ground ginger and pile it into the center of the dough.

6 Turn in the edges of the dough circle all the way around. Brush the surface of the dough with the egg white and sprinkle with the crushed sugar lumps.

7 Bake in a preheated oven, 400°F/200°C, for 35 minutes or until golden-brown. Transfer the pie to a serving plate and serve warm.

NUTRITION
Calories *229*; Sugars *13 g*; Protein *4 g*; Carbohydrate *30 g*; Fat *11 g*; Saturates *7 g*

easy

45 mins

35 mins

🍴 COOK'S TIP

If the pie dough breaks when shaping it into a circle, don't panic—just patch and seal, as the overall effect of this tart is quite rough.

This attractive, French upside-down apple tart is always a popular choice for a comforting dessert.

Apple Tart Tatin

1 Heat the butter and sugar in a 9-inch/23-cm ovenproof skillet over medium heat for about 5 minutes until the mixture starts to caramelize. Remove the pan from the heat.

2 Arrange the apple fourths, skin side down, in the pan, taking care as the butter and sugar will be very hot. Place the skillet back on the heat and let simmer for 2 minutes.

3 Roll out the pie dough on a lightly floured surface to form a circle just a little larger than the skillet.

4 Place the pie dough over the apples, press down, and carefully tuck in the edges to seal the apples under the layer of pie dough.

5 Bake in a preheated oven, 400°F/200°C, for 20–25 minutes until the pie dough is golden. Remove from the oven and let cool for about 10 minutes.

6 Place a serving plate over the skillet and invert so the dough forms the bottom of the tart. Serve warm with plain yogurt.

SERVES **8**

generous ½ cup butter
scant ⅔ cup superfine sugar
4 eating apples, cored and cut into fourths
9 oz/250 g ready-made unsweetened pie dough, thawed if frozen
all-purpose flour, for dusting
plain yogurt, to serve

NUTRITION
Calories *340*; Sugars *23 g*; Protein *2 g*;
Carbohydrate *37 g*; Fat *22 g*; Saturates *12 g*

⭐⭐ easy
🕐 15 mins
🕐 30 mins

🍳 **COOK'S TIP**

Replace the apples with pears, if you prefer. Leave the skin on the pears, cut them into fourths, then remove the core.

This is an old-fashioned dessert, which delights people time after time. It is very quick to make if you use ready-made pastry.

Treacle Tart

SERVES 8

9 oz/250 g ready-made unsweetened pie dough, thawed if frozen
all-purpose flour, for dusting
1 cup light corn syrup
scant 2 cups fresh white bread crumbs
½ cup heavy cream
finely grated zest of ½ lemon or orange
2 tbsp lemon or orange juice
custard or light cream, to serve (optional)

1 Roll out the pie dough on a lightly floured surface and use to line an 8-inch/20-cm loose-bottom tart pan. Set aside the dough trimmings. Prick the bottom of the pie dough with a fork and let chill in the refrigerator.

2 Cut out small shapes from the reserved dough trimmings, such as leaves, stars, or hearts, to decorate the top of the tart.

3 Mix the light corn syrup, bread crumbs, heavy cream, grated lemon or orange zest, and lemon or orange juice together in a bowl.

4 Pour the mixture into the tart shell and decorate the edges of the tart with the dough cut-outs.

5 Bake in a preheated oven, 375°F/190°C, for 35–40 minutes or until the filling is just set.

6 Let the tart cool slightly in the pan. Turn out and onto a serving plate and serve hot or cold with custard or light cream, if desired.

NUTRITION
Calories *378*; Sugars *36 g*; Protein *4 g*;
Carbohydrate *57 g*; Fat *17 g*; Saturates *8 g*

easy

50 mins

40 mins

🍮 **COOK'S TIP**

Use the pie dough trimmings to create a decorative lattice pattern on top of the tart, if you prefer

This is a variation of the classic lemon tart—in this recipe fresh bread crumbs are used to create a much thicker texture.

Orange Tart

1 To make the dough, sift the flour into a bowl and add the sugar. Add the butter and rub it in with your fingertips until the mixture resembles bread crumbs. Add the water and mix to form a soft dough. Wrap in plastic wrap and let chill in the refrigerator for 30 minutes.

2 Roll out the dough on a lightly floured surface to a circle and use to line a 9½-inch/24-cm loose-bottom tart pan. Prick the dough with a fork and let chill in the refrigerator for 30 minutes.

3 Line the tart shell with foil and baking beans and bake in a preheated oven, 375°F/190°C, for 15 minutes. Remove the foil and beans and cook for another 15 minutes.

4 To make the filling, mix the orange zest and juice and the bread crumbs together in a bowl. Stir in the lemon juice and cream. Melt the butter and sugar in a small pan over low heat. Remove the pan from the heat, add the 2 egg yolks, a pinch of salt, and the bread crumb mixture, and stir.

5 Whisk the egg whites with a pinch of salt in a clean bowl until they form soft peaks. Fold them into the egg yolk mixture.

6 Pour the filling into the prepared tart shell and bake in a preheated oven, 325°F/160°C, for about 45 minutes or until just set. Let cool slightly and serve warm with a spoonful of whipped cream decorated with a few strips of orange peel.

SERVES **6 – 8**

sweet pie dough
1¼ cups all-purpose flour, plus extra
    for dusting
2 tbsp superfine sugar
½ cup butter, cut into small pieces
1 tbsp water

filling
grated zest of 2 oranges, plus extra for
    decoration
scant ⅔ cup orange juice
scant 1 cup fresh white bread crumbs
2 tbsp lemon juice
⅔ cup light cream
4 tbsp butter
¼ cup superfine sugar
2 eggs, separated
salt
whipped cream, to serve
strips of orange

NUTRITION
Calories *450*; Sugars *17 g*; Protein *6 g*;
Carbohydrate *40 g*; Fat *31 g*; Saturates *19 g*

⭐⭐   easy

🕐   1 hr 20 mins

🕐   1 hr 45 mins

This frangipane tart, made with fresh cranberries, is ideal for Thanksgiving. If you wish, brush the warm tart with melted apricot jelly.

Apricot *and* Cranberry Tart

SERVES 8

sweet pie dough
1¼ cups all-purpose flour, plus extra
  for dusting
2 tbsp superfine sugar
½ cup butter, cut into small pieces
1 tbsp water

filling
scant 1 cup unsalted butter
1 cup superfine sugar
1 egg
2 egg yolks
⅓ cup all-purpose flour, sifted
1⅔ cups ground almonds
4 tbsp heavy cream
14½ oz/410 g canned apricot halves, drained
generous 1 cup fresh cranberries

NUTRITION
Calories 752; Sugars 40 g; Protein 9 g;
Carbohydrate 59 g; Fat 55 g; Saturates 28 g

✪✪✪ moderate
🕐 1 hr 20 mins
🕐 1 hr 30 mins

1 To make the dough, sift the flour into a bowl and add the sugar. Add the butter and rub it in with your fingertips until the mixture resembles bread crumbs. Add the water and mix to form a soft dough. Wrap in plastic wrap and let chill in the refrigerator for 30 minutes.

2 Roll out the dough on a lightly floured surface and use to line a 9½-inch/ 24-cm loose-bottom tart pan. Prick the dough with a fork and let chill in the refrigerator for 30 minutes.

3 Line the tart shell with foil and baking beans and bake in a preheated oven, 375°F/190°C, for 15 minutes. Remove the foil and baking beans and cook for another 10 minutes.

4 To make the filling, cream the butter and sugar together in a bowl until light and fluffy. Beat in the egg and egg yolks, then stir in the flour, ground almonds, and cream.

5 Place the apricot halves and cranberries on the bottom of the tart shell and spoon the filling over the top.

6 Bake in the preheated oven for about 1 hour or until the topping is just set. Let cool slightly, then serve warm or cold.

These creamy cheese desserts are so delicious that it is hard to believe that they are low in fat— a healthy and tasty option.

Almond Cheesecakes

1 Place the cookies in a clean plastic bag, seal the bag, and using a rolling pin, crush them into small pieces.

2 Place the amaretti crumbs in a bowl and stir in the egg white to bind them together.

3 Arrange 4 non-stick pastry rings or poached egg rings, 3½ inches/9 cm across, on a cookie sheet lined with baking parchment. Divide the amaretti mixture into 4 equal portions and spoon it into the rings, pressing it down well. Bake in a preheated oven, 350°F/180°C, for about 10 minutes until crisp. Remove from the oven and let cool in the rings.

4 Beat the soft cheese, then beat in the almond extract, lime zest, ground almonds, sugar, and golden raisins until well mixed.

5 Dissolve the gelatin in the boiling water and stir in the lime juice. Fold into the cheese mixture and spoon over the amaretti bases. Smooth over the tops and let chill in the refrigerator for 1 hour or until set.

6 Loosen the cheesecakes from the rings with a small spatula and transfer to serving plates. Decorate with slivered toasted almonds and strips of lime peel and serve.

SERVES 4

12 amaretti cookies
1 egg white, beaten lightly
1 cup skim-milk soft cheese
½ tsp almond extract
½ tsp finely grated lime zest
scant ¼ cup ground almonds
2 tbsp superfine sugar
⅓ cup golden raisins
2 tsp powdered gelatin
2 tbsp boiling water
2 tbsp lime juice

to decorate
2 tbsp slivered toasted almonds
strips of lime peel

NUTRITION
Calories *361*; Sugars *29 g*; Protein *16 g*;
Carbohydrate *43 g*; Fat *15 g*; Saturates *4 g*

⭐⭐   easy

🕐   1 hr 15 mins

🕐   10 mins

This simple combination of fudgy meringue topped with mascarpone and raspberries is the perfect finale to any meal.

Brown Sugar Pavlovas

SERVES 4

2 large egg whites
1 tsp cornstarch
1 tsp raspberry vinegar
½ cup light brown sugar, crushed free of lumps
2 tbsp red currant jelly
2 tbsp unsweetened orange juice
¾ cup lowfat mascarpone cheese
1 cup raspberries, thawed if frozen
rose-scented geranium leaves, to decorate (optional)

1 Line a large cookie sheet with baking parchment. Whisk the egg whites until very stiff and dry. Gently fold in the cornstarch and vinegar.

2 Gradually whisk in the sugar, a spoonful at a time, until the mixture is thick and glossy.

3 Divide the mixture into 4 portions and spoon onto the prepared cookie sheet, spaced well apart. Smooth each portion into a circle, 4 inches/10 cm in diameter, and bake in a preheated oven, 300°F/150°C, for 40–45 minutes until lightly browned and crisp. Remove from the oven and let cool on the cookie sheet.

4 Place the red currant jelly and orange juice in a small saucepan and heat, stirring constantly, until melted. Let cool for 10 minutes.

5 Using a spatula, carefully remove each pavlova from the baking parchment and transfer to 4 serving plates. Top with the mascarpone and the raspberries. Glaze the fruit with the red currant jelly and orange glaze, and decorate with the geranium leaves, if using.

NUTRITION

Calories 155; Sugars 34 g; Protein 5 g; Carbohydrate 35 g; Fat 0.2 g; Saturates 0 g

easy

1 hr

1 hr

🍴 COOK'S TIP

Make a large pavlova by forming the meringue into a 7-inch/18-cm circle on a lined cookie sheet. Bake in a preheated oven for 1 hour.

This simple recipe is easy to prepare and cook, and is deliciously warming. For a healthy treat, serve hot on a pool of lowfat custard.

Baked Pears *with* Cinnamon

1 Core and peel the pears, then slice them in half lengthwise, and brush all over with the lemon juice to prevent them from turning brown. Arrange the pears, cored side down, in a small non-stick roasting pan.

2 Place the sugar, cinnamon, and lowfat spread in a small pan and heat gently, stirring constantly, until the sugar has dissolved. Keep the heat as low as possible to stop too much water evaporating from the lowfat spread as it gets hot. Spoon the mixture over the pears.

3 Bake in a preheated oven, 400°F/200°C, for 20–25 minutes or until the pears are tender and golden, occasionally spooning the sugar mixture over the fruit during the cooking time.

4 To serve, heat the custard until piping hot and spoon a little over the bases of 4 warmed serving plates. Arrange 2 pear halves on each plate.

5 Decorate the pears with a little grated lemon peel and serve with custard.

SERVES 4

4 ripe pears
2 tbsp lemon juice
¼ cup light brown sugar
1 tsp ground cinnamon
5 tbsp lowfat spread
lowfat custard, to serve
finely grated lemon peel, to decorate
lowfat custard, to serve

NUTRITION

Calories *207*; Sugars *35 g*; Protein *3 g*;
Carbohydrate *37 g*; Fat *6 g*; Saturates *2 g*

⭐⭐   easy

🕐   10 mins

🕐   25 mins

🍮 COOK'S TIP

For alternative flavors, replace the cinnamon with ground ginger and serve the pears sprinkled with chopped preserved ginger in syrup. Alternatively, use ground allspice and spoon over some warmed dark rum to serve.

The orange-flavored cream can be prepared well in advance, but do not make up the banana parcels until just before you need to bake them.

Baked Bananas

S E R V E S 4

4 bananas
2 passion fruit
4 tbsp orange juice
4 tbsp orange-flavored liqueur

orange-flavored cream
²⁄₃ cup heavy cream
3 tbsp confectioners' sugar
2 tbsp orange-flavored liqueur

1 To make the orange-flavored cream, pour the cream into a large bowl and sprinkle over the confectioners' sugar. Whisk the mixture until it is standing in soft peaks. Carefully fold in the orange-flavored liqueur and let chill in the refrigerator until required.

2 Peel the bananas and place each one on a sheet of foil.

3 Cut the passion fruit in half and squeeze the juice of each half over each banana. Spoon over the orange juice and liqueur.

4 Fold the foil over the top of the bananas, tucking the ends in so they are completely enclosed.

5 Bake the bananas in a preheated oven, 350°F/180°C, for about 10 minutes or until the bananas are just tender and piping hot. Check by piercing the foil parcel with a toothpick.

6 Transfer the foil parcels to warmed serving plates. Open out the foil parcels at the table and serve immediately with the chilled orange-flavored cream.

N U T R I T I O N
Calories *380* Sugars *40 g*; Protein *2 g*;
Carbohydrate *43 g*; Fat *18 g*; Saturates *11 g*

easy

30 mins

10 mins

🏅 **C O O K ' S T I P**

Leave the bananas in their skins for a really quick dessert. Split the banana skins and pop in 1–2 cubes of chocolate. Wrap the bananas in foil and bake in a preheated oven for 10 minutes, or until the chocolate just melts.

This winter dessert is a classic dish. Large, fluffy apples are hollowed out and filled with spices, almonds, and blackberries.

Baked Apples *with* Berries

1 Using a small, sharp knife, make a shallow cut through the skin around the center of each apple—this will help the apples to cook through.

2 Core the apples, brush the centers with the lemon juice to prevent them from turning brown, and stand them in an ovenproof dish.

3 Mix the blackberries, almonds, allspice, lemon peel, and sugar together in a bowl. Using a teaspoon, spoon the mixture into the center of each apple.

4 Pour the port into the dish, add the cinnamon stick, and bake the apples in a preheated oven, 400°F/200°C, for 35–40 minutes or until tender and softened.

5 Drain the cooking juices into a small pan and set over low heat. Keep the apples warm.

6 Discard the cinnamon from the cooking juices and add the cornstarch mixture to the pan. Cook, stirring constantly, until thickened.

7 Heat the custard in a small pan until piping hot. Pour the sauce over the apples and serve with the custard.

SERVES 4

4 medium-size cooking apples
1 tbsp lemon juice
1 cup prepared blackberries, thawed if frozen
1 tbsp slivered almonds
½ tsp ground allspice
½ tsp finely grated lemon peel
2 tbsp raw brown sugar
1¼ cups ruby port
1 cinnamon stick, broken
2 tsp cornstarch blended with 2 tbsp cold water
lowfat custard, to serve

NUTRITION
Calories *228*; Sugars *31 g*; Protein *1 g*; Carbohydrate *31 g*; Fat *2 g*; Saturates *0.2 g*

easy

10 mins

50 mins

This rich dessert is cooked with cream and apples and delicately flavored with orange.

Italian Bread Pudding

SERVES 4

1 tbsp butter, for greasing
2 small eating apples, peeled, cored, and sliced into rings
generous ⅓ cup granulated sugar
2 tbsp white wine
3½ oz/100 g bread, sliced with crusts removed (slightly stale French baguette is ideal)
1¼ cups light cream
2 eggs, beaten
pared peel of 1 orange, cut into thin sticks

1 Lightly grease a 5-cup/1.2-litre deep ovenproof dish with the butter.

2 Arrange the apple rings in the bottom of the dish and sprinkle over half of the sugar.

3 Pour the wine over the apples. Add the bread slices, pushing them down with your hands to flatten them slightly.

4 Mix the cream, eggs, the remaining sugar, and the orange peel together in a small bowl, then pour the mixture over the bread. Let soak for 30 minutes.

5 Bake the dessert in a preheated oven, 350°F/180°C, for 25 minutes or until golden and set. Remove from the oven, let cool slightly and serve warm.

NUTRITION
Calories *387*; Sugars *31 g*; Protein *8 g*; Carbohydrate *45 g*; Fat *20 g*; Saturates *12 g*

⭐⭐ easy

🕐 45 mins

🕐 25 mins

🍳 **COOK'S TIP**

For a variation, try adding dried fruit, such as apricots, cherries, or dates, to the dessert.

These baked mini-ricotta desserts are delicious served warm or chilled and will keep in the refrigerator for 3–4 days.

Tuscan Pudding

1 Lightly grease 4 mini ovenproof bowls or ramekin dishes with the butter.

2 Put the dried fruit in a bowl and cover with warm water. Let soak for about 10 minutes.

3 Beat the ricotta cheese and the egg yolks together in a bowl. Stir in the superfine sugar, cinnamon, and orange zest and mix well.

4 Drain the dried fruit in a strainer set over a bowl. Mix the drained fruit with the ricotta cheese mixture.

5 Spoon the mixture into the prepared bowls or ramekin dishes.

6 Bake in a preheated oven, 350°F/180°C, for 15 minutes. The tops should just be firm to the touch, but should have not turned brown.

7 Decorate the desserts with grated orange zest. Serve warm or chilled with a spoonful of crème fraîche or whipped cream, if desired.

SERVES 4

1 tbsp butter, for greasing
²⁄₃ cup mixed dried fruit
generous 1 cup ricotta cheese
3 egg yolks
¼ cup superfine sugar
1 tsp cinnamon
finely grated zest of 1 orange, plus extra
   to decorate
crème fraîche or whipped cream, to serve
   (optional)

NUTRITION
Calories 293; Sugars 28 g; Protein 9 g;
Carbohydrate 28 g; Fat 17 g; Saturates 9 g

⭐⭐   easy
🥄   20 mins
🕐   15 mins

👨‍🍳 **COOK'S TIP**

Crème fraîche has a slightly sour, nutty taste and is very thick. It is suitable for cooking, but has the same fat content as heavy cream. It can be made by stirring cultured buttermilk into heavy cream and refrigerating overnight.

The mascarpone gives this baked cheesecake a wonderfully tangy flavor. Ricotta cheese could be used as an alternative.

Mascarpone Cheesecake

SERVES 8

4 tbsp unsalted butter, plus extra for greasing
3 cups ginger cookie crumbs
1 tablespoon chopped preserved ginger
2¼ cups mascarpone cheese
finely grated zest and juice of 2 lemons
½ cup superfine sugar
2 large eggs, separated
fruit coulis (see Cook's Tip), to serve

1 Grease a 10-inch/25-cm springform cake pan or loose-bottom pan with butter and line the bottom with baking parchment.

2 Melt the butter in a pan over low heat and stir in the crushed cookies and chopped ginger. Use the mixture to line the pan, pressing the mixture about ¼ inch/5 mm up the sides.

3 Beat the mascarpone cheese, lemon zest and juice, sugar, and egg yolks together in a bowl until quite smooth.

4 Whisk the egg whites in a clean bowl until stiff, then fold into the cheese and lemon mixture.

5 Pour the mixture into the prepared pan and bake in a preheated oven, 350°F/ 180°C, for 35–45 minutes until just set. Don't worry if it cracks or sinks—this is quite normal. Leave the cheesecake to cool in the pan. Serve with a fruit coulis (see Cook's Tip).

NUTRITION
Calories 327; Sugars 25 g; Protein 9 g;
Carbohydrate 33 g; Fat 18 g; Saturates 11 g

⭐⭐⭐   moderate
🕐   15 mins
🕔   50 mins

👩‍🍳 **COOK'S TIP**

Fruit coulis can be made by cooking 14 oz/400 g fruit, such as blueberries, for 5 minutes with 2 tablespoons of water. Strain the mixture, then stir in about 1 tablespoon of sifted confectioners' sugar. Let cool before serving.

These unusual and scrumptious little parcels are the perfect dessert for anyone with a sweet tooth.

Baked Sweet Ravioli

1 To make the sweet pasta dough, sift the flour into a large bowl, then add the butter, sugar, and 3 of the eggs and mix well.

2 Mix the yeast and warm milk together in a small bowl and when thoroughly combined, mix into the dough.

3 Knead the dough for 20 minutes, cover with a clean cloth, and set aside in a warm place for 1 hour to rise.

4 To make the filling, mix the chestnut paste, cocoa, sugar, almonds, crushed amaretti cookies, and orange marmalade together in a bowl.

5 Grease a large cookie sheet with some butter.

6 Roll out the pasta dough on a lightly floured surface into a thin sheet and cut into 2-inch/5-cm circles with a plain dough cutter.

7 Put a spoonful of filling onto each circle and then fold in half, pressing the edges to seal. Transfer the ravioli to the prepared cookie sheet, spacing them out well.

8 Beat the remaining egg and brush all over the ravioli to glaze. Bake in a preheated oven, 350°F/180°C, for 20 minutes. Serve hot.

SERVES 4

pasta
3³⁄₄ cups all-purpose flour, plus extra for dusting
²⁄₃ cup butter, plus extra for greasing
³⁄₄ cup superfine sugar
4 eggs
1 oz/25 g yeast
¹⁄₂ cup lukewarm milk

filling
²⁄₃ cup chestnut paste
¹⁄₂ cup unsweetened cocoa
generous ¹⁄₄ cup superfine sugar
¹⁄₂ cup chopped almonds
1 cup crushed amaretti cookies
generous ¹⁄₂ cup orange marmalade

NUTRITION
Calories 765; Sugars 56 g; Protein 16 g; Carbohydrate 114 g; Fat 30 g; Saturates 15 g

✪✪✪ moderate
🕐 1 hr 30 mins
🕐 20 mins

Cakes *and* Bread

There is nothing more traditional than afternoon tea and cakes and this chapter gives a wickedly extravagant twist to some of those delicious teatime classics—full of chocolate, spice, and all things nice, these recipes are a treat to enjoy. The chapter includes a variety of different cakes depending on the time you have and the effort you want to spend. Small cakes include Cranberry Muffins, Almond Slices, and Molasses Biscuits. These cakes are easier to prepare and cook than larger ones and are particular favorites.

These popular snacks are ideal split in half and toasted, then spread with butter. A luxury mix of dried fruit gives them a rich taste.

Teacakes

MAKES 12 TEACAKES

2 tbsp butter, cut into small pieces, plus extra for greasing
3½ cups white bread flour, plus extra for dusting
1 envelope active dry yeast
¼ cup superfine sugar
1 tsp salt
1¼ cups lukewarm milk
½ cup luxury dried fruit mix
1–2 tbsp honey, for brushing

1 Grease several cookie sheets with a little butter.

2 Sift the flour into a large bowl. Stir in the dried yeast, sugar, and salt. Add the butter and rub it in with your fingertips until the mixture resembles fine bread crumbs. Add the milk and mix to form a soft dough.

3 Knead the dough on a lightly floured surface for 5 minutes. Alternatively, use an electric mixer with a dough hook.

4 Place the dough in a greased bowl, cover, and let rise in a warm place for about 1–1½ hours or until the dough has doubled in size.

5 Knead the dough again for a few minutes and knead in the fruit. Divide the dough into 12 circles and place on the prepared cookie sheets. Cover and let stand for another 1 hour or until springy to the touch.

6 Bake in a preheated oven, 400°F/200°C, for 20 minutes.

7 Transfer the teacakes to a wire rack and brush with the honey while they are still warm. Let cool before serving them split in half, toasted if desired.

NUTRITION
Calories *197*; Sugars *11 g*; Protein *6 g*;
Carbohydrate *39 g*; Fat *3 g*; Saturates *2 g*

★★ easy
◔ 3 hrs 15 mins
🕐 20 mins

 COOK'S TIP

It is important to have the milk at the right temperature: heat it until you can put your little finger into the milk and leave it there for 10 seconds without it feeling too hot.

These cinnamon-flavored buns are delicious if they are served a few minutes after they come out of the oven.

Cinnamon Swirls

1 Grease a 9-inch/23-cm square baking pan with a little butter.

2 Sift the flour and salt into a large bowl. Stir in the dried yeast. Add the butter and rub it in with your fingertips until the mixture resembles fine bread crumbs. Add the egg and milk and mix to form a dough.

3 Place the dough in a greased bowl, cover, and let stand in a warm place for about 40 minutes or until the dough has doubled in size.

4 Punch down the dough lightly for about 1 minute, then roll out on a lightly floured surface to a rectangle 12 x 9 inches/30 x 23 cm.

5 To make the filling, cream the butter, cinnamon, and brown sugar together in a bowl until light and fluffy. Spread the filling over the dough rectangle, leaving a 1-inch/2.5-cm border all around. Sprinkle over the currants.

6 Roll up the dough from one of the long edges, and press down to seal. Cut the roll into 12 slices. Place them in the prepared pan, cover, and let stand for 30 minutes.

7 Bake in a preheated oven, 375°F/190°C, for 20–30 minutes or until well risen. Brush the swirls with the syrup and let cool slightly before serving warm.

MAKES 12 BUNS

2 tbsp butter, cut into small pieces, plus extra for greasing
generous 1½ cups white bread flour, plus extra for dusting
½ tsp salt
1 envelope active dry yeast
1 egg, beaten lightly
½ cup lukewarm milk
2 tbsp maple syrup

filling
4 tbsp butter, softened
2 tsp ground cinnamon
¼ cup brown sugar
⅓ cup currants

NUTRITION
Calories *160*; Sugars *10 g*; Protein *4 g*;
Carbohydrate *24 g*; Fat *6 g*; Saturates *4 g*

⭐⭐⭐   moderate

🕐   1 hr 25 mins

🕐   30 mins

This spicy, fruit tea bread is quick and easy to make. Serve it buttered and with a drizzle of honey for an afternoon snack.

Cinnamon *and* Currant Loaf

MAKES 1 LOAF

⅔ cup butter, cut into small pieces, plus extra for greasing
2¾ cups all-purpose flour
pinch of salt
1 tbsp baking powder
1 tbsp ground cinnamon
¾ cup brown sugar
¾ cup currants
finely grated peel of 1 orange
5–6 tbsp orange juice
6 tbsp milk
2 eggs, beaten lightly

1 Grease a 2-lb/900-g loaf pan and line the bottom with baking parchment.

2 Sift the flour, salt, baking powder, and ground cinnamon into a large bowl. Add the butter and rub it in with your fingertips until the mixture resembles coarse bread crumbs.

3 Stir in the sugar, currants, and orange peel. Beat the orange juice, milk, and eggs together and add to the dry ingredients. Mix well.

4 Spoon the mixture into the prepared pan. Make a slight dip in the center of the mixture to help it rise evenly.

5 Bake in a preheated oven, 350°F/180°C, for about 1–1 hour 10 minutes or until a toothpick or the point of a sharp knife inserted into the center of the loaf comes out clean.

6 Let the loaf cool in the pan before transferring to a wire rack to cool before slicing and serving.

NUTRITION
Calories *439*; Sugars *33 g*; Protein *7 g*; Carbohydrate *67 g*; Fat *18 g*; Saturates *11 g*

  moderate

1 hr 10 mins

1 hr 10 mins

COOK'S TIP

Once you have added the liquid to the dry ingredients, work as quickly as possible, because the baking powder is activated by the liquid.

This fruity bread is excellent for afternoon tea or morning coffee time with its moist texture and delicious flavor.

Banana *and* Date Loaf

1 Grease a 2-lb/900-g loaf pan with a little butter and line the bottom with baking parchment.

2 Sift the flour into a large bowl. Add the butter and rub it in with your fingertips until the mixture resembles fine bread crumbs.

3 Stir in the sugar, chopped dates, bananas, beaten eggs, and honey and mix together to form a soft, dropping consistency.

4 Spoon the mixture into the prepared loaf pan, spreading it out evenly. Smooth the surface with the back of a knife.

5 Bake the loaf in a preheated oven, 325°F/160°C, for about 1 hour or until golden-brown on top and a toothpick or the point of a sharp knife inserted into the center of the loaf comes out clean.

6 Let the loaf cool in the pan before turning out and transferring to a wire rack to cool completely.

7 Serve the loaf, cut into thick slices with a few fresh dates, if desired.

MAKES 1 LOAF

⅓ cup butter, cut into small pieces, plus extra for greasing
generous 1½ cups self-rising flour
⅓ cup superfine sugar
⅔ cup chopped pitted dates
2 bananas, mashed coarsely
2 eggs, beaten lightly
2 tbsp honey
fresh dates, to serve (optional)

COOK'S TIP

This fruity bread will keep for several days if stored in an airtight container and kept in a cool, dry place.

NUTRITION
Calories *432*; Sugars *41 g*; Protein *7 g*; Carbohydrate *70 g*; Fat *16 g*; Saturates *10 g*

⭐⭐⭐ moderate

15 mins

1 hr

This bread is full of good things—chopped dates, sesame seeds, and honey. Toast thick slices and spread with soft cheese for a light snack.

Date *and* Honey Loaf

MAKES 1 LOAF

1–2 tbsp butter, for greasing
1¾ cups white bread flour, plus extra
    for dusting
½ cup brown bread flour
½ tsp salt
1 envelope active dry yeast
generous ¾ cup lukewarm water
3 tbsp corn oil
3 tbsp honey
½ cup chopped pitted dates
2 tbsp sesame seeds

1 Grease a 2-lb/900-g loaf pan with butter. Sift the flours into a large bowl, and stir in the salt and dried yeast.

2 Pour in the water, corn oil, and honey and mix to form a dough.

3 Knead the dough on a lightly floured surface for 5 minutes or until smooth.

4 Place the dough in a greased bowl, cover, and let rise in a warm place for about 1 hour or until doubled in size.

5 Knead in the chopped dates and sesame seeds. Shape the dough and place in the pan.

6 Cover and let stand in a warm place for another 30 minutes or until springy to the touch.

7 Bake in a preheated oven, 425°F/220°C, for 30 minutes or until a hollow sound is heard when the bottom of the loaf is tapped.

8 Transfer the loaf to a wire rack and let cool completely. Serve cut into slices.

NUTRITION
Calories *240*; Sugars *14 g*; Protein *6 g*;
Carbohydrate *44 g*; Fat *6 g*; Saturates *1 g*

⭐⭐⭐   moderate
🕐   2 hrs 40 mins
🕐   30 mins

👨‍🍳 **COOK'S TIP**

If you cannot find a warm place, sit a bowl with the dough in it over a pan of warm water and cover.

The pumpkin paste in this loaf makes it beautifully moist. It is delicious eaten at any time of the day.

Pumpkin Loaf

1 Grease a 2-lb/900-g loaf pan with vegetable oil.

2 Chop the pumpkin into large pieces and wrap in buttered foil. Cook in a preheated oven, 400°F/200°C, for 30–40 minutes or until tender.

3 Let the pumpkin cool completely before mashing well with a fork to make a thick paste.

4 Cream the butter and sugar together in a bowl until light and fluffy. Add the beaten eggs, a little at a time.

5 Stir in the pumpkin paste. Fold in the flour, baking powder, salt, and allspice.

6 Fold the pumpkin seeds gently through the mixture, then spoon into the prepared loaf pan.

7 Bake in a preheated oven, 325°F/160°C, for about 1¼–1½ hours or until a toothpick or the point of a sharp knife inserted into the center of the loaf comes out clean.

8 Transfer the loaf to a wire rack to cool, then serve.

MAKES 1 LOAF

1 tbsp vegetable oil, for greasing
1 lb/450 g pumpkin flesh
½ cup butter, softened
¾ cup superfine sugar
2 eggs, beaten lightly
generous 1½ cups all-purpose flour, sifted
1½ tsp baking powder
½ tsp salt
1 tsp ground allspice
2 tbsp pumpkin seeds

NUTRITION
Calories *456*; Sugars *33 g*; Protein *7 g*;
Carbohydrate *62 g*; Fat *21 g*; Saturates *12 g*

easy

1 hr 30 mins

2 hrs 10 mins

COOK'S TIP

To ensure that the pumpkin paste is dry, place it in a pan over medium heat for a few minutes, stirring frequently, until it thickens.

The flavors in this bread will bring a touch of sunshine to your breakfast table. The mango can be replaced with other dried fruits, if desired.

Tropical Fruit Bread

MAKES 1 LOAF

2 tbsp butter, cut into small pieces, plus extra for greasing
2½ cups white bread flour, plus extra for dusting
5 tbsp bran
½ tsp salt
½ tsp ground ginger
1 envelope active dry yeast
2 tbsp brown sugar
1 cup lukewarm water
½ cup candied pineapple, chopped finely
2 tbsp finely chopped dried mango
½ cup shredded coconut, toasted
1 egg, beaten lightly
2 tbsp shredded coconut

1 Grease a cookie sheet with butter. Sift the flour into a large bowl. Stir in the bran, salt, ginger, dried yeast, and sugar. Add the butter and rub it in with your fingertips, then add the water, and mix to form a dough.

2 Knead the dough on a lightly floured surface for 5–8 minutes or until smooth. Alternatively, use an electric mixer with a dough hook. Place the dough in a greased bowl, cover, and let rise in a warm place for 30 minutes or until the dough has doubled in size.

3 Knead the pineapple, mango, and toasted coconut into the dough. Shape into a circle and place on the cookie sheet. Score the top with the back of a knife. Cover and let stand in a warm place for another 30 minutes.

4 Brush the loaf with the beaten egg and sprinkle with the 2 tablespoons of shredded coconut. Bake in a preheated oven, 425°F/220°C, for 30 minutes or until golden-brown on top.

5 Remove the loaf from the oven and transfer to a wire rack to cool before serving in slices.

NUTRITION
Calories *228*; Sugars *10 g*; Protein *6 g*; Carbohydrate *37 g*; Fat *7 g*; Saturates *5 g*

 moderate

1 hr 15 mins

30 mins

COOK'S TIP

To test the bread after the second rising, gently poke the dough with your finger—it should spring back if it has risen enough.

This sweet loaf is delicately flavored with citrus fruits. As with Tropical Fruit Bread (see opposite), it is excellent served at breakfast time.

Citrus Bread

1 Lightly grease a cookie sheet with a little butter.

2 Sift the flour and salt into a large bowl. Stir in the sugar and dried yeast. Add the butter and rub it in with your fingertips until the mixture resembles bread crumbs. Add the orange, lemon, and lime juice, and water and mix to form a dough.

3 Knead the dough on a lightly floured surface for 5 minutes. Alternatively, use an electric mixer with a dough hook. Place the dough in a greased bowl, cover, and let rise in a warm place for 1 hour or until doubled in size.

4 Meanwhile, grate the peel of the orange, lemon, and lime. Knead the fruit peels into the dough.

5 Divide the dough into 2 balls, making one slightly bigger than the other. Place the larger ball on the cookie sheet and set the smaller one on top.

6 Push a floured finger through the center of the dough. Cover and let rise for about 40 minutes or until springy to the touch.

7 Bake in a preheated oven, 425°F/220°C, for 35 minutes. Remove from the oven and transfer to a wire rack. Glaze with honey and let cool.

MAKES 1 LOAF

4 tbsp butter, cut into small pieces, plus extra for greasing
3½ cups white bread flour, plus extra for dusting
½ tsp salt
¼ cup superfine sugar
1 envelope active dry yeast
5–6 tbsp orange juice
4 tbsp lemon juice
3–4 tbsp lime juice
⅔ cup lukewarm water
1 orange
1 lemon
1 lime
2 tbsp honey

NUTRITION
Calories *195*; Sugars *10 g*; Protein *5 g*; Carbohydrate *37 g*; Fat *4 g*; Saturates *2 g*

⭐⭐⭐   moderate
🕐   1 hr 55 mins
🕐   35 mins

For the chocoholics among us, this bread is not only great fun to make, it is even better to eat.

Chocolate Bread

MAKES 1 LOAF

1 tbsp butter, for greasing
3½ cups white bread flour, plus extra for greasing
¼ cup unsweetened cocoa
1 tsp salt
1 envelope active dry yeast
2 tbsp brown sugar
1 tbsp oil
1¼ cups lukewarm water
butter curls, to serve

1 Lightly grease a 2-lb/900-g loaf pan with a little butter.

2 Sift the flour and unsweetened cocoa into a large bowl. Stir in the salt, dried yeast, and brown sugar.

3 Pour in the oil along with the water and mix together to form a dough.

4 Knead the dough on a lightly floured surface for 5 minutes. Alternatively, use an electric mixer with a dough hook.

5 Place the dough in a greased bowl, cover, and let rise in a warm place for about 1 hour or until the dough has doubled in size.

6 Punch down the dough and shape it into a loaf. Place the dough in the prepared pan, cover, and let rise in a warm place for another 30 minutes.

7 Bake in a preheated oven, 400°F/200°C, for 25–30 minutes or until a hollow sound is heard when the bottom of the bread is tapped.

8 Transfer the bread to a wire rack and let cool completely. Cut into slices and serve with butter.

NUTRITION
Calories *228*; Sugars *4 g*; Protein *8 g*;
Carbohydrate *46 g*; Fat *3 g*; Saturates *1 g*

⭐⭐⭐   moderate
🕙   2 hrs 40 mins
🕐   30 mins

👨‍🍳 **COOK'S TIP**

This bread can be sliced and spread with butter or it can be lightly toasted.

This is a sweet bread, which has mango paste mixed into the dough, resulting in a moist loaf with an exotic flavor.

Mango Twist Bread

1 Grease a cookie sheet with a little butter. Sift the flour and salt into a large bowl. Stir in the yeast, ground ginger, and brown sugar. Add the butter and rub it in with your fingertips until the mixture resembles bread crumbs. Stir in the mango paste, lukewarm water, and honey and mix to form a dough.

2 Knead the dough on a lightly floured surface for about 5 minutes or until smooth. Alternatively, use an electric mixer with a dough hook. Place the dough in a greased bowl, cover, and let rise in a warm place for 1 hour or until the dough has doubled in size.

3 Knead in the golden raisins and shape the dough into 2 sausage shapes, each 10 inches/25 cm long. Carefully twist the 2 pieces together and pinch the ends to seal. Place the dough on the prepared cookie sheet, cover, and let rise in a warm place for another 40 minutes.

4 Brush the loaf with the egg and bake in a preheated oven, 425°F/220°C, for 30 minutes or until golden-brown. Transfer the loaf to a wire rack and let cool. Dust with confectioners' sugar before serving.

MAKES 1 LOAF

3 tbsp butter, cut into small pieces, plus extra for greasing
3½ cups white bread flour, plus extra for dusting
1 tsp salt
1 envelope active dry yeast
1 tsp ground ginger
¼ cup brown sugar
1 small mango, peeled, pitted, and blended to a paste
1 cup lukewarm water
2 tbsp honey
⅔ cup golden raisins
1 egg, beaten lightly
confectioners' sugar, for dusting

NUTRITION

Calories *228*; Sugars *18 g*; Protein *6 g*; Carbohydrate *46 g*; Fat *4 g*; Saturates *2 g*

⭐⭐⭐   moderate

🕐   2 hrs 50 mins

🕐   30 mins

🍴 COOK'S TIP

You can tell when the bread is cooked as it will sound hollow when tapped on the bottom.

It is worth using a good quality olive oil for this cake as this will determine its flavor. The cake will keep very well in an airtight container.

Olive Oil, Fruit, *and* Nut Cake

SERVES 8

1 tbsp butter, for greasing
generous 1½ cups self-rising flour
¼ cup superfine sugar
½ cup milk
4 tbsp orange juice
⅔ cup olive oil
½ cup mixed dried fruit
¼ cup pine nuts

1 Lightly grease a 7-inch/18-cm cake pan with a little butter and line with baking parchment.

2 Sift the flour into a large bowl and stir in the superfine sugar. Make a well in the center of the dry ingredients and pour in the milk and orange juice. Stir the batter with a wooden spoon, gradually beating in the flour and the sugar.

3 Pour in the olive oil, stirring well so that all of the ingredients are evenly and thoroughly mixed. Stir the mixed dried fruit and pine nuts into the mixture and spoon it into the prepared pan, spreading it out evenly. Smooth the surface with a knife.

4 Bake in a preheated oven, 350°F/180°C, for about 45 minutes or until the cake is golden and firm to the touch.

5 Let the cake cool in the pan for a few minutes before transferring to a wire rack to cool completely. Serve the cake warm or cold and cut into slices.

NUTRITION
Calories *309*; Sugars *17 g*; Protein *4 g*;
Carbohydrate *38 g*; Fat *17 g*; Saturates *3 g*

moderate

10 mins

45 mins

🍳 **COOK'S TIP**

Pine nuts are best known as the flavoring ingredient in the classic Italian pesto, but here they give a delicate, slightly resinous flavor to this cake.

This cake is flavored with clementine zest and juice, creating a very rich buttery cake but one full of fresh fruit flavor.

Clementine Cake

1 Grease a 7-inch/18-cm round pan with butter and line the bottom with baking parchment.

2 Pare the zest from the clementines and chop it finely. Cream the butter, sugar, and clementine zest together in a bowl until pale and fluffy.

3 Gradually add the beaten eggs to the mixture, beating thoroughly after each addition.

4 Gently fold in the flour, ground almonds, and cream. Spoon the batter into the prepared pan.

5 Bake in a preheated oven, 350°F/180°C, for about 55–60 minutes or until a toothpick or the point of a sharp knife inserted into the center of the cake comes out clean. Remove from the oven and let cool slightly.

6 Meanwhile, make the glaze. Put the clementine juice into a pan with the superfine sugar. Bring to a boil over low heat and let simmer for 5 minutes.

7 Turn out the cake onto a wire rack. Drizzle the glaze over the cake until it has been absorbed and sprinkle with the sugar lumps. Let cool completely, then serve in slices.

COOK'S TIP

If you prefer, chop the zest from the clementines in a food processor or blender along with the sugar at Step 2. Tip the mixture into a bowl with the butter and start to cream the mixture.

SERVES 8

¾ cup butter, softened, plus extra
   for greasing
2 clementines
¾ cup superfine sugar
3 eggs, beaten lightly
1¼ cups self-rising flour
3 tbsp ground almonds
3 tbsp light cream

glaze and topping
6 tbsp clementine juice
2 tbsp superfine sugar
3 white sugar lumps, crushed

NUTRITION
Calories *427*; Sugars *32 g*; Protein *6 g*;
Carbohydrate *48 g*; Fat *25 g*; Saturates *13 g*

★★★   moderate
🕐   10 mins
🕐   1 hr 5 mins

Cornmeal adds texture to this fruitcake, as well as a golden yellow color. It also acts as a flour, binding the ingredients together.

Crunchy Fruitcake

SERVES 8

⅓ cup butter, softened, plus extra for greasing
½ cup superfine sugar
2 eggs, beaten lightly
generous ⅓ cup self-rising flour, sifted
1 tsp baking powder
⅔ cup cornmeal
1⅓ cups mixed dried fruit
¼ cup pine nuts
grated zest of 1 lemon
4 tbsp lemon juice
2 tbsp milk

1 Grease a 7-inch/18-cm cake pan with a little butter and line the bottom with baking parchment.

2 Cream the butter and sugar together in a bowl until light and fluffy.

3 Gradually add the beaten eggs, a little at a time, beating well after each addition. Gently fold the flour, baking powder, and cornmeal into the batter until well blended.

4 Stir in the mixed dried fruit, pine nuts, grated lemon zest, lemon juice, and milk. Spoon the batter into the prepared pan and smooth the surface.

5 Bake in a preheated oven, 350°F/180°C, for 1 hour or until a toothpick or the point of a sharp knife inserted into the center of the cake comes out clean.

6 Remove from the oven and let the cake cool in the pan before turning out onto a wire rack to cool completely. Cut into slices and serve.

NUTRITION
Calories 328; Sugars 33 g; Protein 59 g; Carbohydrate 47 g; Fat 15 g; Saturates 7 g

moderate

5–10 mins

1 hr

COOK'S TIP

To give a crumblier and lighter fruit cake, omit the cornmeal and use generous 1 cup self-rising flour instead.

Baking in a deep, fluted kugelhopf pan ensures that you create a cake with a stunning shape. The moist cake is full of fresh orange flavor.

Orange Kugelhopf Cake

1 Grease and flour a 10-inch/25-cm kugelhopf pan or deep ring mold.

2 Cream the butter and superfine sugar together in a bowl until light and fluffy. Add the egg yolks, one at a time, whisking well after each addition.

3 Sift the flour, a pinch of salt, and baking powder into a separate bowl. Using a metal spoon, fold the dry ingredients and the orange juice alternately into the creamed mixture, as lightly as possible. Stir in the orange flower water and orange zest.

4 Whisk the egg whites in a clean bowl until they form soft peaks, then gently fold them into the batter.

5 Pour into the prepared pan or mold and bake in a preheated oven, 350°F/ 180°C, for 50–55 minutes or until a toothpick or the point of a sharp knife inserted into the center of the cake comes out clean.

6 Put the orange juice and sugar in a small pan and bring to a boil over low heat, then let simmer for 5 minutes until the sugar has dissolved.

7 Remove the cake from the oven and let cool in the pan for 10 minutes. Prick the top of the cake with a toothpick and brush over half of the syrup. Let the cake cool, still in the pan, for another 10 minutes. Invert the cake onto a wire rack placed over a deep plate and brush the syrup over the cake until it is covered. Serve warm or cold.

SERVES 6 – 8

1 cup butter, softened, plus extra for greasing
generous 1 cup superfine sugar
4 eggs, separated
scant 3½ cups all-purpose flour
3 tsp baking powder
1¼ cups fresh orange juice
1 tbsp orange flower water
1 tsp grated orange zest
salt

syrup
¾ cup orange juice
1 cup granulated sugar

NUTRITION
Calories *877*; Sugars *82 g*; Protein *12 g*; Carbohydrate *137 g*; Fat *35 g*; Saturates *21 g*

⭐⭐⭐⭐ challenging
🌀 25 mins
🕐 55 mins

The addition of pieces of fresh apple and crunchy almonds to the cake mixture makes this beautifully moist yet with a crunch to it.

Spiced Apple Ring

SERVES 8

3/4 cup butter, softened, plus extra
   for greasing
3/4 cup superfine sugar
3 eggs, beaten lightly
1 1/4 cups self-rising flour
1 tsp ground cinnamon
1 tsp ground allspice
2 eating apples, cored and grated
2 tbsp apple juice or milk
1/4 cup slivered almonds

1 Lightly grease a 10-inch/25-cm ovenproof ring mold with butter.

2 Cream the butter and sugar together in a bowl until light and fluffy. Gradually add the beaten eggs, beating well after each addition.

3 Sift the flour and spices, then fold them into the creamed mixture.

4 Stir in the grated apples and the apple juice or milk, and mix to a soft dropping consistency.

5 Sprinkle the slivered almonds around the bottom of the mold and spoon the batter on top. Smooth the surface with the back of the spoon.

6 Bake in a preheated oven, 350°F/180°C, for about 30 minutes until well risen and a toothpick or the point of a sharp knife inserted into the center of the cake comes out clean.

7 Let the cake cool in the pan before turning out and transferring to a wire rack to cool completely. Serve the spiced apple ring cut into slices.

NUTRITION
Calories 379; Sugars 27 g; Protein 5 g;
Carbohydrate 43 g; Fat 22 g; Saturates 13 g

★★★   moderate
🕐   1 hr 5 mins
🕐   30 mins

 COOK'S TIP

This cake can also be made in a 7-inch/18-cm round cake pan if you do not have an ovenproof ring mold.

This cake has a moist coffee sponge cake on the bottom, covered with a deliciously crisp crunchy, spicy topping.

Coffee Streusel Cake

1 Grease a 9-inch/23-cm loose-bottom round cake pan with butter and line with baking parchment. Sift the flour and baking powder into a large bowl, then stir in the superfine sugar.

2 Whisk the milk, eggs, butter, and coffee mixture together in a separate bowl and pour onto the dry ingredients. Add the chopped almonds and mix lightly together. Spoon the batter into the prepared pan.

3 To make the topping, mix the flour and raw brown sugar together in a large bowl. Add the butter and rub in with your fingertips until the mixture is crumbly. Sprinkle in the allspice and the water and bring the mixture together in loose crumbs. Sprinkle the topping evenly over the cake.

4 Bake in a preheated oven, 375°F/190°C, for about 1 hour. Cover loosely with foil if the top starts to brown too quickly. Remove from the oven and let the cake cool in the pan, then turn out onto a wire rack to cool completely. Dust with confectioners' sugar just before serving.

SERVES 8

1 tbsp butter, for greasing
2 cups all-purpose flour
1 tbsp baking powder
1/3 cup superfine sugar
2/3 cup milk
2 eggs
1/2 cup butter, melted and cooled
2 tbsp instant coffee mixed with
    1 tbsp boiling water
1/3 cup chopped almonds
confectioners' sugar, for dusting

topping
1/2 cup self-rising flour
1/3 cup raw brown sugar
2 tbsp butter, cut into small pieces
1 tsp ground allspice
1 tbsp water

NUTRITION
Calories *409*; Sugars *21 g*; Protein *8 g*;
Carbohydrate *55 g*; Fat *19 g*; Saturates *10 g*

⭐⭐⭐   moderate
        10 mins
        1 hr

This cake is full of flavor from the mixed fruits. The fruit gives the cake its sweetness so there is no need for extra sugar.

Sugar-Free Fruitcake

SERVES 8

½ cup butter, cut into small pieces, plus extra for greasing
2½ cups all-purpose flour
2 tsp baking powder
1 tsp ground allspice
⅓ cup no-soak dried apricots, chopped
½ cup chopped pitted dates
⅓ cup candied cherries, chopped
⅔ cup raisins
½ cup milk
2 eggs, beaten lightly
grated peel of 1 orange
5–6 tbsp orange juice
3 tbsp honey

1 Grease an 8-inch/20-cm round cake pan with a little butter and line the bottom with baking parchment.

2 Sift the flour, baking powder, and allspice together into a large bowl. Add the butter and rub it in with your fingertips until the mixture resembles fine bread crumbs.

3 Carefully stir in the apricots, dates, candied cherries, and raisins with the milk, beaten eggs, grated orange peel, and orange juice.

4 Stir in the honey and mix together to form a soft dropping consistency. Spoon into the prepared cake pan and smooth the surface.

5 Bake in a preheated oven, 350°F/180°C, for 1 hour until a toothpick or the point of a sharp knife inserted into the center of the cake comes out clean.

6 Remove from the oven and let the cake cool in the pan before turning out.

NUTRITION
Calories *423*; Sugars *34 g*; Protein *8 g*;
Carbohydrate *68 g*; Fat *16 g*; Saturates *9 g*

★★★   moderate
🕐   1 hr 5 mins
🕐   1 hr

 COOK'S TIP

For a fruity alternative, replace the honey with 1 mashed ripe banana.

This spicy gingerbread is made even moister and more delicious by the addition of chopped fresh apples.

Gingerbread

1 Lightly grease a 9-inch/23-cm square cake pan with a little butter and line with baking parchment.

2 Melt the butter, sugar, and molasses in a pan over low heat. Remove the pan from the heat and let cool.

3 Sift the flour, baking powder, baking soda, and ginger into a large bowl. Stir in the milk, beaten egg, and cooled buttery liquid, followed by the chopped apples coated with the lemon juice.

4 Mix together gently, then pour the batter into the prepared pan.

5 Bake in a preheated oven, 325°F/160°C, for 30–35 minutes or until the cake has risen and a toothpick or the point of a sharp knife inserted into the center of the cake comes out clean.

6 Remove from the oven and let the cake cool in the pan before turning out and cutting into 12 bars.

MAKES 12 BARS

⅔ cup butter, plus extra for greasing
scant 1 cup brown sugar
2 tbsp molasses
generous 1½ cups all-purpose flour
1 tsp baking powder
2 tsp baking soda
2 tsp ground ginger
⅔ cup milk
1 egg, beaten lightly
2 eating apples, peeled, chopped, and coated with 1 tbsp lemon juice

NUTRITION
Calories *248*; Sugars *21 g*; Protein *3 g*;
Carbohydrate *36 g*; Fat *11 g*; Saturates *7 g*

⭐⭐⭐   moderate
🕐   1 hr 15 mins
🕐   35 mins

👨‍🍳 **COOK'S TIP**

If you enjoy the flavor of ginger, try adding 1 tablespoon finely chopped preserved ginger to the mixture at Step 3.

These biscuits are very light and buttery like traditional biscuits, but they have a deliciously rich flavor, which comes from the molasses.

Molasses Biscuits

MAKES 8 BISCUITS

6 tbsp butter, cut into small pieces, plus extra for greasing
generous 1½ cups self-rising flour, plus extra for dusting
1 tbsp superfine sugar
pinch of salt
1 eating apple, peeled, cored, and chopped
1 egg, beaten lightly
2 tbsp molasses
5 tbsp milk

1 Lightly grease a cookie sheet with a little butter.

2 Sift the flour, sugar, and a pinch of salt into a large bowl.

3 Add the butter and rub it in with your fingertips until the mixture resembles fine bread crumbs.

4 Stir the chopped apple into the mixture until well blended.

5 Mix the beaten egg, molasses, and milk together in a pitcher. Add to the dry ingredients and mix well to form a soft dough.

6 Roll out the dough on a lightly floured surface to a thickness of about ¾ inch/2 cm and cut out 8 circles, using a 2-inch/5-cm cutter.

7 Arrange the biscuits on the prepared cookie sheet and bake in a preheated oven, 425°F/220°C, for about 8–10 minutes.

8 Transfer the biscuits to a wire rack and let cool slightly. Serve split in half and spread with butter.

NUTRITION
Calories 208; Sugars 9 g; Protein 4 g; Carbohydrate 30 g; Fat 9 g; Saturates 6 g

★★★ moderate
15 mins
10 mins

COOK'S TIP

These biscuits can be frozen, but are best thawed and eaten within 1 month.

These are an alternative to traditional biscuits, using sweet candied cherries, which not only create color but add a distinct flavor.

Cherry Biscuits

1 Lightly grease a cookie sheet with a little butter.

2 Sift the flour, sugar, and salt into a large bowl. Add the butter and rub it in with your fingertips until the mixture resembles bread crumbs.

3 Stir in the candied cherries and golden raisins, then add the beaten egg.

4 Set aside 1 tablespoon of the milk for glazing, then add the remainder to the mixture. Mix well to form a soft dough.

5 Roll out the dough on a lightly floured surface to a thickness of about ¾ inch/2 cm and cut out 8 circles, using a 2-inch/5-cm cutter.

6 Place the biscuits on the prepared cookie sheet and brush the tops with the reserved milk.

7 Bake in a preheated oven, 425°F/220°C, for 8–10 minutes or until the biscuits are golden-brown.

8 Transfer the biscuits to a wire rack and let cool slightly. Serve split and spread with butter.

COOK'S TIP

These biscuits will freeze very successfully, but they are best thawed and eaten within 1 month.

MAKES 8 BISCUITS

6 tbsp butter, cut into small pieces, plus extra for greasing
generous 1½ cups self-rising flour, plus extra for dusting
1 tbsp superfine sugar
pinch of salt
3 tbsp candied cherries, chopped
3 tbsp golden raisins
1 egg, beaten lightly
scant ¼ cup milk

NUTRITION
Calories 211; Sugars 10 g; Protein 4 g;
Carbohydrate 31 g; Fat 9 g; Saturates 6 g

very easy

10 mins

10 mins

These savory muffins are an ideal accompaniment to soup, or they make a tasty alternative to sweet cakes for serving with coffee.

Cranberry Muffins

MAKES 18 MUFFINS

1 tbsp butter, for greasing
generous 1½ cups all-purpose flour
2 tsp baking powder
½ tsp salt
¼ cup superfine sugar
4 tbsp butter, melted
2 eggs, beaten lightly
generous ¾ cup milk
1 cup fresh cranberries
scant ½ cup freshly grated Parmesan cheese

1 Lightly grease 2 muffin pans with a little butter. Sift the flour, baking powder, and salt into a large bowl. Stir in the superfine sugar.

2 Mix the butter, beaten eggs, and milk together in a separate bowl, then pour into the bowl of dry ingredients. Mix lightly until evenly blended. Stir in the fresh cranberries.

3 Divide the mixture among the prepared pans. Sprinkle the grated Parmesan cheese over the top of each muffin.

4 Bake in a preheated oven, 400°F/200°C, for about 20 minutes or until the muffins are well risen and golden-brown.

5 Remove from the oven and let the muffins cool slightly in the pans. Transfer to a wire rack and let cool completely before serving.

NUTRITION

Calories 96; Sugars 4 g; Protein 3 g;
Carbohydrate 14 g; Fat 4 g; Saturates 2 g

moderate

1 hr 5 mins

20 mins

👨‍🍳 COOK'S TIP

For a sweet alternative to this recipe, replace the Parmesan cheese with raw brown sugar at Step 6, if you prefer.

The sugar lumps give a lovely crunchy taste to this easy-to-make, light cake, which is ideal to serve with cream for a dessert.

Crispy-Topped Fruit Bake

1 Grease a 2-lb/900-g loaf pan with butter and line with baking parchment. Core, peel, and finely dice the apples. Place them in a pan with the lemon juice, bring to a boil over low heat, cover, and let simmer for 10 minutes or until softened and pulpy. Beat well and let cool.

2 Sift the flour, baking powder, and 1 teaspoon of cinnamon into a bowl, adding any bran remaining in the sifter. Stir in 2/3 cup of the blackberries and the light brown sugar.

3 Make a well in the center of the ingredients and add the egg, yogurt, and cooled apple paste. Mix well to incorporate thoroughly. Spoon the batter into the prepared loaf pan and smooth the surface.

4 Sprinkle with the remaining blackberries, pressing them down into the cake, and top with the sugar lumps. Bake in a preheated oven, 375°F/190°C, for 40–45 minutes. Remove from the oven and let cool in the pan.

5 Remove the cake from the pan and peel away the baking parchment. Serve dusted with cinnamon and decorated with extra blackberries and apple slices.

SERVES 10

1 tbsp butter, for greasing
12 oz/350 g cooking apples
3 tbsp lemon juice
generous 2 cups whole-wheat self-rising flour
½ tsp baking powder
1 tsp ground cinnamon, plus extra for dusting
1 cup prepared blackberries, thawed if frozen, plus extra to decorate
scant 1 cup light brown sugar
1 egg, beaten lightly
¾ cup lowfat plain yogurt
2 oz/55 g white or brown sugar lumps, lightly crushed
sliced eating apple, to decorate

COOK'S TIP

Try replacing the blackberries with blueberries. Use the canned or frozen variety if fresh blueberries are unavailable.

NUTRITION
Calories 227; Sugars 30 g; Protein 5 g; Carbohydrate 53 g; Fat 1 g; Saturates 0.2 g

⭐⭐ easy
🕐 15 mins
🕐 1 hr

Serve this moist, fruit-laden cake for a special occasion. It would also make an excellent Thanksgiving cake.

Rich Fruitcake

1 tbsp butter, for greasing
generous ½ cup no-soak dried prunes
1 cup chopped pitted dates
generous ¾ cup unsweetened orange juice
2 tbsp molasses
1 tsp finely grated lemon zest
1 tsp finely grated orange zest
generous 1½ cups whole-wheat self-rising flour
1 tsp mixed spice
⅔ cup seedless raisins
⅔ cup golden raisins
⅔ cup currants
⅔ cup dried cranberries
3 large eggs, separated

to decorate

1 tbsp apricot jelly, warmed
confectioners' sugar, for dusting
generous 1 cup sugarpaste
strips of orange zest
strips of lemon zest

NUTRITION
Calories 772; Sugars 137 g; Protein 14 g;
Carbohydrate 179 g; Fat 5 g; Saturates 1 g

⭐⭐⭐   moderate
🕐   35 mins
🕐   1 hr 45 mins

1 Grease a deep round 8-inch/20-cm cake pan with butter and line with baking parchment. Chop the prunes, place in a pan with the dates, pour over the orange juice and let simmer over low heat for 10 minutes. Remove the pan from the heat and beat the fruit mixture to a paste. Add the molasses and lemon and orange zest. Let cool.

2 Sift the flour and mixed spice into a large bowl, adding any bran remaining in the sifter. Add the dried fruits. When the prune mixture is cool, whisk in the egg yolks.

3 Whisk the egg whites in a clean bowl until stiff. Spoon the fruit mixture into the dry ingredients and mix together.

4 Using a metal spoon, gently fold in the egg whites. Transfer to the prepared cake pan and bake in a preheated oven, 325°F/160°C, for 1½ hours. Remove from the oven and let the cake cool in the pan.

5 Remove the cake from the pan and brush the top with jelly. Dust the surface with confectioners' sugar and roll out the sugarpaste thinly. Lay the sugarpaste over the top of the cake and trim the edges. Decorate with orange and lemon zest and serve.

This melt-in-the-mouth version of a favorite cake has a fraction of the fat of the traditional cake, making it a wonderfully healthy treat.

Carrot *and* Ginger Cake

1 Lightly grease an 8-inch/20-cm round cake tin with butter or lowfat spread and line with baking parchment.

2 Sift the flour, baking powder, baking soda, ground ginger, and salt into a bowl. Stir in the sugar, carrots, preserved ginger, fresh gingerroot, and raisins. Beat the eggs, corn oil, and orange juice together, then pour into the bowl. Mix well.

3 Spoon the batter into the prepared pan and bake in a preheated oven, 350°F/180°C, for 1–1¼ hours until firm to the touch, or until a toothpick or the point of a sharp knife inserted into the center of the cake comes out clean. Remove from the oven and let the cake cool in the pan.

4 To make the frosting, place the soft cheese in a bowl and beat to soften. Sift in the confectioners' sugar and add the vanilla extract. Mix well.

5 Remove the cooled cake from the pan and smooth the frosting over the top. Decorate the cake with grated carrot, chopped preserved ginger, and ground ginger, then serve.

COOK'S TIP

If you prefer a nuttier cake, substitute the raisins for chopped walnuts or, add 2 tablespoons raisins and 2 tablespoons chopped walnuts at Step 2.

SERVES 10

1 tbsp butter or lowfat spread, for greasing
generous 1½ cups all-purpose flour
1 tsp baking powder
1 tsp baking soda
2 tsp ground ginger
½ tsp salt
scant 1 cup light brown sugar
generous 1 cup grated carrots
2 pieces preserved ginger, chopped
1 tablespoon grated fresh gingerroot
⅓ cup seedless raisins
2 eggs, beaten lightly
3 tbsp corn oil
juice of 1 orange
frosting
1 cup lowfat soft cheese
4 tbsp confectioners' sugar
1 tsp vanilla extract
to decorate
grated carrot
finely chopped preserved ginger
ground ginger

NUTRITION
Calories *249*; Sugars *28 g*; Protein *7 g*; Carbohydrate *46 g*; Fat *6 g*; Saturates *1 g*

⭐⭐⭐   moderate
🕐   15 mins
🕐   1 hr 15 mins

Serve this moist, light sponge cake rolled up with a creamy almond and strawberry filling for a delicious treat.

Strawberry Roulade

SERVES 8

3 large eggs
⅔ cup superfine sugar
scant 1 cup all-purpose flour
1 tbsp hot water

filling
¾ cup lowfat mascarpone cheese
1 tsp almond extract
1½ cups small strawberries

to decorate
1 tbsp slivered almonds, toasted
1 tsp confectioners' sugar
a few strawberries

NUTRITION
Calories *166*; Sugars *19 g*; Protein *6 g*;
Carbohydrate *30 g*; Fat *3 g*; Saturates *1 g*

✪✪✪✪ challenging
🕐 30 mins
🕐 10 mins

1 Line a 14 x 10-inch/35 x 25-cm jelly roll pan with baking parchment. Place the eggs in a heatproof bowl with the superfine sugar. Place the bowl over a pan of hot, but not boiling water and whisk until pale and thick.

2 Remove the bowl from the pan. Sift in the flour and fold into the eggs along with the hot water. Pour the batter into the pan and bake in a preheated oven, 425°F/220°C, for 8–10 minutes or until golden and set.

3 Turn out the sponge cake onto a sheet of baking parchment. Peel off the lining paper and roll up the sponge cake tightly along with the baking parchment. Wrap in a dish cloth and let cool.

4 Mix the mascarpone cheese and almond extract together in a small bowl. Set aside a few strawberries for decoration, then wash, hull, and slice the rest. Chill the mascarpone mixture and the strawberries in the refrigerator until required.

5 Unroll the sponge cake, spread the mascarpone mixture over the surface, and sprinkle with the sliced strawberries. Carefully roll the sponge cake up again and transfer to a large serving plate. Sprinkle with almonds and dust with confectioners' sugar. Decorate with the reserved strawberries.

This is a great family favorite and is perfect served with afternoon tea or eaten as a light snack.

Coconut Cake

1 Grease a 2-lb/900-g loaf pan with a little butter and line the bottom with baking parchment.

2 Sift the flour and a pinch of salt into a large bowl. Add the butter and rub it in with your fingertips until the mixture resembles fine bread crumbs.

3 Stir in the raw brown sugar, shredded coconut, eggs, and milk and mix to a soft dropping consistency.

4 Spoon the batter into the prepared pan and smooth the surface with a spatula. Bake in a preheated oven, 325°F/160°C, for 30 minutes.

5 Remove the cake from the oven and sprinkle with the extra coconut. Return the cake to the oven and bake for another 30 minutes, or until well risen and golden and a toothpick or the point of a sharp knife inserted into the center of the cake comes out clean.

6 Remove from the oven and let the cake cool slightly in the pan before turning out and transferring to a wire rack to cool completely. Serve in slices.

SERVES 6 – 8

½ cup butter, cut into small pieces, plus extra for greasing
generous 1½ cups self-rising flour
½ cup raw brown sugar
1 cup shredded coconut, plus extra for sprinkling
2 eggs, beaten lightly
4 tbsp milk
salt

NUTRITION
Calories *464*; Sugars *20 g*; Protein *8 g*; Carbohydrate *54 g*; Fat *26 g*; Saturates *18 g*

⭐ very easy
🕐 10 mins
🕐 30 mins

🎩 **COOK'S TIP**

The flavor of this cake is enhanced by storing it in a cool dry place for a few days before eating.

A mouthwatering dessert that is sure to impress your guests, especially if it is served with lots of whipped cream.

Almond Slices

SERVES 8

3 eggs
²⁄₃ cup ground almonds
1½ cups milk powder
1 cup granulated sugar
½ tsp saffron strands
scant ½ cup sweet butter
1 tbsp slivered almonds, to decorate
whipped cream, to serve (optional)

1 Beat the eggs together in a bowl.

2 Place the ground almonds, milk powder, sugar, and saffron in a large bowl and stir to mix well.

3 Melt the butter in a small pan over low heat. Pour the melted butter over the dry ingredients and mix well until thoroughly combined.

4 Add the reserved beaten eggs to the batter and stir to blend well.

5 Spread the batter in a shallow 6–8-inch/15–20-cm ovenproof dish and bake in a preheated oven, 325°F/160°C, for 45 minutes. Test whether the cake is cooked through by piercing with a toothpick or the point of a sharp knife—it will come out clean if the cake is cooked thoroughly.

6 Cut the almond cake into slices. Decorate the almond slices with slivered almonds, and transfer to serving plates. Serve hot or cold with whipped cream, if liked .

NUTRITION
Calories *416*; Sugars *37 g*; Protein *11 g*;
Carbohydrate *38 g*; Fat *26 g*; Saturates *12 g*

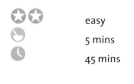

easy
5 mins
45 mins

🍽 **COOK'S TIP**

These almond slices are best eaten hot, but they may also be served cold. They can be made a day or even a week in advance and reheated. They also freeze very well.

This variation of traditional Irish soda bread is best eaten the same day it has been baked, still warm from the oven.

Soda Bread

1 Grease a cookie sheet with butter and dust lightly with flour.

2 Sift the flours, baking powder, baking soda, sugar, and salt into a large bowl and add any bran remaining in the sifter.

3 Beat the egg and yogurt together in a pitcher and pour the mixture into the dry ingredients. Mix together to make a soft and sticky dough.

4 Knead the dough on a lightly floured surface for a few minutes until smooth, then shape the dough into a round about 2-inches/5-cm deep.

5 Transfer the dough to the prepared cookie sheet. Using a knife, mark a cross shape in the center of the top of the dough.

6 Bake in a preheated oven, 375°F/190°C, for about 40 minutes or until the bread is golden-brown.

7 Transfer the loaf to a wire rack and let cool. Cut into slices to serve.

MAKES 1 LOAF

1 tbsp butter, for greasing
generous 2 cups all-purpose flour, plus extra for dusting
generous 2 cups whole-wheat flour
2 tsp baking powder
1 tsp baking soda
2 tbsp superfine sugar
1 tsp salt
1 egg, beaten lightly
generous 1¾ cups unsweetened yogurt

NUTRITION
Calories *203*; Sugars *7 g*; Protein *8 g*;
Carbohydrate *42 g*; Fat *2 g*; Saturates *0 g*

⭐⭐⭐   moderate
🕐   1 hr 10 mins
🕐   40 mins

👨‍🍳 COOK'S TIP

For a fruity version of this soda bread, add ¾ cup of raisins to the dry ingredients at step 2.

Serve this spicy bread fresh from the oven with your favorite soup or a fresh tomato and onion salad for a light lunch.

Spicy Bread

MAKES 1 LOAF

2 tbsp butter, cut into small pieces, plus extra for greasing
generous 1½ cups self-rising flour
¾ cup all-purpose flour
1 tsp baking powder
¼ tsp salt
¼ tsp cayenne pepper
2 tsp curry powder
2 tsp poppy seeds
⅔ cup milk
1 egg, beaten lightly

1 Grease a cookie sheet with a little butter.

2 Sift both flours into a large bowl along with the baking powder, salt, cayenne, curry powder, and poppy seeds.

3 Add the butter and rub it in with your fingertips until the mixture resembles bread crumbs. Add the milk and beaten egg and mix to from a soft dough.

4 Knead the dough on a lightly floured surface for a few minutes. Shape the dough into a circle and, using a sharp knife, mark a cross shape in the center of the top.

5 Bake in a preheated oven, 375°F/190°C, for 45 minutes.

6 Transfer the bread to a wire rack and let cool. Serve in chunks or slices.

NUTRITION
Calories *122*; Sugars *1 g*; Protein *4 g*;
Carbohydrate *22 g*; Fat *3 g*; Saturates *2 g*

★★★ moderate
1 hr 10 mins
45 mins

COOK'S TIP

If the bread looks as though it is browning too much, cover it with a piece of foil for the remainder of the cooking time.

This Mexican-style corn bread makes a great accompaniment to chile con carne or it can be eaten on its own as a tasty snack.

Chile Corn Bread

1 Grease an 8-inch/20-cm square cake pan with butter and line the bottom with baking parchment.

2 Sift the flour, cornmeal, baking powder, and salt into a large bowl.

3 Add the green chile and scallions to the dry ingredients and mix well.

4 Beat the eggs together with the sour cream and corn oil in a pitcher. Pour the mixture into the bowl of dry ingredients and mix quickly. Pour the batter into the prepared cake pan.

5 Bake in a preheated oven, 400°F/200°C, for 20–25 minutes or until the loaf has risen and is lightly browned on top.

6 Let the bread cool slightly before turning out of the pan. Cut into bars or squares to serve.

MAKES 12 SQUARES

1 tbsp butter, for greasing
generous 1½ cups all-purpose flour
1 cup cornmeal
1 tbsp baking powder
½ tsp salt
1 fresh green chile, seeded and finely chopped
5 scallions, chopped finely
2 eggs
generous ½ cup sour cream
½ cup corn oil

NUTRITION
Calories 179; Sugars 1 g; Protein 3 g; Carbohydrate 10 g; Fat 14 g; Saturates 3 g

⭐⭐   easy
🕐   5 mins
🕐   25 mins

👨‍🍳 **COOK'S TIP**

Add ¾ cup of corn kernels to the mixture at Step 3, if you prefer.

This is a quick bread to make. It is full of cheesy flavor and, to enjoy it at its best, it should be eaten as fresh as possible.

Cheese *and* Chive Bread

SERVES 8

1 tbsp butter, for greasing
generous 1½ cups self-rising flour
1 tsp salt
1 tsp mustard powder
1 cup grated sharp cheese
2 tbsp chopped fresh chives
1 egg, beaten lightly
2 tbsp butter, melted
⅔ cup milk

1 Grease a 9-inch/23-cm square cake pan with butter and line the bottom with baking parchment.

2 Sift the flour, salt, and mustard powder into a large bowl.

3 Set aside 3 tablespoons of the grated sharp cheese for sprinkling over the top of the loaf before baking in the oven.

4 Stir the remaining cheese into the bowl along with the chives. Mix well.

5 Add the beaten egg, melted butter, and milk to the dry ingredients and stir the mixture thoroughly to combine.

6 Pour the batter into the prepared pan, spreading it out evenly. Smooth the surface with a knife, then sprinkle over the reserved grated cheese.

7 Bake in a preheated oven, 375°F/190°C, for about 30 minutes.

8 Remove from the oven and let the bread cool slightly in the pan, then turn out onto a wire rack to cool completely. Cut into triangles to serve.

NUTRITION
Calories *190*; Sugars *1 g*; Protein *7 g*;
Carbohydrate *22 g*; Fat *9 g*; Saturates *5 g*

★★★   moderate
        25 mins
        30 mins

🍳 **COOK'S TIP**

You can use any hard, sharp cheese of your choice for this recipe.

This bread is not at all like the store-bought, ready-made garlic bread. Instead it has a subtle flavor and a soft texture.

Garlic Bread Rolls

1 Grease a cookie sheet with a little butter.

2 Place the garlic cloves and milk in a pan, bring to a boil over low heat, and let simmer for 15 minutes. Remove the pan from the heat and let cool slightly, then process in a blender or food processor to blend in the garlic.

3 Sift the flour and salt into a large bowl and stir in the yeast and mixed herbs.

4 Add the garlic-flavored milk, corn oil, and beaten egg to the dry ingredients and mix to form a dough.

5 Knead the dough on a lightly floured surface for a few minutes until smooth and soft.

6 Place the dough in a greased bowl, cover, and let rise in a warm place for about 1 hour or until doubled in size.

7 Punch down the dough by kneading it for 2 minutes. Divide the dough into 8 pieces and shape into rolls. Place the rolls on the prepared cookie sheet. Score the top of each roll with a knife, cover, and let stand for 15 minutes.

8 Brush the rolls with milk and sprinkle rock salt over the top.

9 Bake in a preheated oven, 425°F/220°C, for 15–20 minutes. Transfer the rolls to a wire rack and let cool before serving.

MAKES **8** ROLLS

1 tbsp butter, for greasing
12 garlic cloves, peeled
1½ cups milk
3½ cups white bread flour, plus extra
    for dusting
1 tsp salt
1 envelope active dry yeast
1 tbsp dried mixed herbs
2 tbsp corn oil
1 egg, beaten lightly
milk, for brushing
rock salt, for sprinkling

NUTRITION
Calories *265*; Sugars *3 g*; Protein *10 g*;
Carbohydrate *46 g*; Fat *6 g*; Saturates *2 g*

easy

1 hr 45 mins

35 mins

This is a delicious Italian bread made with olive oil. The topping of red onions and thyme is particularly flavorsome.

Mini Focaccia

SERVES 4

2 tbsp olive oil, plus extra for brushing
2½ cups white bread flour, plus extra
    for dusting
½ tsp salt
1 envelope active dry yeast
1 cup lukewarm water
1 cup pitted green or black olives, halved

topping
2 red onions, sliced
2 tbsp olive oil
1 tsp sea salt
1 tbsp fresh thyme leaves

NUTRITION
Calories *439*; Sugars *3 g*; Protein *9 g*;
Carbohydrate *71 g*; Fat *15 g*; Saturates *2 g*

⭐⭐   *easy*

🕐   2 hrs 15 mins

🕐   25 mins

1 Lightly brush several cookie sheets with olive oil. Sift the flour and salt into a large bowl, then stir in the yeast. Pour in the olive oil and water and mix to form a dough.

2 Knead the dough on a lightly floured surface for 5 minutes. Alternatively, use an electric mixer with a dough hook.

3 Place the dough in a greased bowl, cover, and let stand in a warm place for about 1–1½ hours or until the dough has doubled in size. Punch down the dough by kneading it again for 1–2 minutes.

4 Knead half of the olives into the dough. Divide the dough into fourths and shape the fourths into circles. Place them on the prepared cookie sheets and push your fingers into the dough to achieve a dimpled effect.

5 To make the topping, sprinkle the red onions and remaining olives over the dough circles. Drizzle the olive oil over the top and sprinkle with the sea salt and thyme leaves. Cover and let rise for 30 minutes.

6 Bake in a preheated oven, 375°F/190°C, for 20–25 minutes or until the focaccia are golden.

7 Transfer to a wire rack and let cool before serving.

These white rolls have the addition of finely chopped sun-dried tomatoes. The tomatoes are sold in jars and are available at most large stores.

Sun-Dried Tomato Rolls

1 Lightly grease a cookie sheet with a little butter. Sift the flour and salt into a large bowl. Stir in the yeast, then pour in the butter, milk, and eggs. Mix to form a dough.

2 Knead the dough on a floured surface for 5 minutes. Alternatively, use an electric mixer with a dough hook.

3 Place the dough in a greased bowl, cover, and let rise in a warm place for 1–1½ hours or until the dough has doubled in size. Punch down the dough for 2–3 minutes.

4 Knead the sun-dried tomatoes into the dough, sprinkling the surface with extra flour, because the tomatoes are quite oily.

5 Divide the dough into 8 equal-size balls and place them on the prepared cookie sheet. Cover and let rise for 30 minutes or until the rolls have doubled in size.

6 Brush the rolls with milk and bake in a preheated oven, 450°F/230°C, for 10–15 minutes or until the rolls are golden-brown.

7 Transfer the rolls to a wire rack and let cool slightly before serving.

🎩 COOK'S TIP

Add some finely chopped anchovies or olives to the dough at Step 4 for extra flavor, if desired.

SERVES 8

1 tbsp butter, for greasing
generous 1½ cups white bread flour, plus extra for dusting
½ tsp salt
1 envelope active dry yeast
⅓ cup butter, melted and cooled slightly
3 tbsp lukewarm milk
2 eggs, beaten lightly
1¾ oz/50 g sun-dried tomatoes, well drained and finely chopped
milk, for brushing

NUTRITION

Calories 214; Sugars 1 g; Protein 5 g; Carbohydrate 22 g; Fat 12 g; Saturates 7 g

⭐⭐ easy
🕐 2 hrs 15 mins
🕐 15 mins

These homemade biscuits are given an interesting flavor by adding grated sharp cheese and mustard to the mixture.

Cheese *and* Mustard Biscuits

MAKES 8 BISCUITS

4 tbsp butter, cut into small pieces, plus extra for greasing
generous 1½ cups self-rising flour, plus extra for dusting
1 tsp baking powder
1¼ cups grated sharp cheese
1 tsp mustard powder
⅔ cup milk
salt and pepper

1 Lightly grease a cookie sheet with a little butter. Sift the flour, baking powder, and a pinch of salt into a large bowl. Add the butter and rub it in with your fingertips until the mixture resembles bread crumbs.

2 Stir in the cheese, mustard powder, and enough milk to form a soft dough.

3 Knead the dough very lightly on a lightly floured surface, then flatten it out with the palm of your hand to a depth of about 1 inch/2.5 cm.

4 Cut the dough into 8 wedges with a knife. Brush each one with a little milk and sprinkle with pepper to taste.

5 Bake in a preheated oven, 425°F/220°C, for 10–15 minutes or until the biscuits are golden-brown.

6 Transfer the biscuits to a wire rack and let cool slightly before serving.

NUTRITION
Calories *218*; Sugars *1 g*; Protein *7 g*;
Carbohydrate *22 g*; Fat *12 g*; Saturates *7 g*

⭐ very easy
🕐 15 mins
🕐 15 mins

🍴 COOK'S TIP

Biscuits should be eaten on the day they are made as they quickly go stale. Serve them split in half and spread with butter.

This flavorsome bread contains only the minimum amount of fat. Serve with a bowl of hot soup for a filling and nutritious light meal.

Savory Bell Pepper Bread

1 Grease a 9-inch/23-cm round springform cake pan. Place the bell pepper halves on a broiler rack and cook under a preheated hot broiler until the skin is charred. Let cool for 10 minutes, peel off the skin, and chop the flesh. Slice the tomatoes into strips, place in a bowl, and pour over the water. Let soak.

2 Place the yeast and sugar in a pitcher, pour over the water, and let stand for 10–15 minutes until frothy. Sift the flour into a bowl and add 1 teaspoon of dried rosemary. Make a well in the center and pour in the yeast mixture.

3 Add the tomato paste, tomatoes and soaking liquid, bell peppers, yogurt, and half the salt. Mix to form a soft dough. Knead the dough on a lightly floured surface for 3–4 minutes until smooth. Place in a floured bowl, cover, and let rise in a warm room for 40 minutes until doubled in size.

4 Knead the dough again and place in the prepared cake pan. Using a wooden spoon, form "dimples" in the surface. Cover and let stand for 30 minutes. Brush with olive oil and sprinkle with rosemary and salt. Bake in a preheated oven, 425°F/220°C, for 35–40 minutes. Remove the loaf from the oven and let cool in the pan for 10 minutes. Release from the pan and let cool on a wire rack before serving.

COOK'S TIP

For a quick, filling snack serve the bread with a bowl of hot soup in winter, or crisp salad greens in summer.

SERVES **4**

1 tbsp butter, for greasing
1 small red bell pepper, halved and seeded
1 small green bell pepper, halved and seeded
1 small yellow bell pepper, halved and seeded
2 oz/55 g dry-package sun-dried tomatoes
scant ¼ cup boiling water
2 tsp dried yeast
1 tsp superfine sugar
⅔ cup lukewarm water
3½ cups white bread flour, plus extra for dusting
2 tsp dried rosemary
2 tbsp tomato paste
⅔ cup lowfat plain yogurt
1 tbsp coarse salt
1 tbsp olive oil

NUTRITION
Calories *468*; Sugars *11 g*; Protein *16 g*; Carbohydrate *97 g*; Fat *5 g*; Saturates *1 g*

✪✪✪✩ challenging
2 hrs
50 mins

Cookies

Nothing can compare with a homemade cookie for bringing a touch of pleasure to a coffee break or teatime. This selection of delicious cookies and after-dinner treats will tantalize your tastebuds and keep you coming back for more. Delicious cookies like Citrus Crescents, Meringues, Rock Drops, and Gingersnaps are quick, easy, and satisfying to make. You can easily vary the ingredients to suit your taste—the possibilities for inventiveness when making cookies are endless and this chapter shows you how.

These savory crackers have a delicious buttery flavor. Make sure you use a sharp cheese for the best flavor.

Cheese Sablés

MAKES 35 CRACKERS

²/₃ cup butter, cut into small pieces, plus extra for greasing
generous 1 cup all-purpose flour, plus extra for dusting
1½ cups grated sharp cheese
1 egg yolk
sesame seeds, for sprinkling

1 Lightly grease several cookie sheets with a little butter.

2 Mix the flour and grated cheese together in a bowl.

3 Add the butter to the cheese and flour mixture and mix with your fingertips until combined.

4 Stir in the egg yolk and mix to form a dough. Wrap the dough in plastic wrap and let chill in the refrigerator for about 30 minutes.

5 Roll out the cheese dough thinly on a lightly floured surface. Cut out 2½-inch/6-cm circles, re-rolling the trimmings to make about 35 circles.

6 Place the dough circles onto the prepared cookie sheets and sprinkle the sesame seeds over the top of them.

7 Bake in a preheated oven, 200°C/400°F, for 20 minutes or until the sablés are lightly golden.

8 Transfer the cheese sablés to a wire rack and let cool slightly before serving.

NUTRITION
Calories 67; Sugars 0 g; Protein 2 g; Carbohydrate 3 g; Fat 5 g; Saturates 3 g

⭐⭐ easy
🕐 50 mins
🕐 20 mins

👨‍🍳 **COOK'S TIP**

Cut out any shape you like for your savory sablés. Children will enjoy them cut into animal or other fun shapes.

Nothing compares with the taste of these freshly baked authentic gingersnaps, which have a lovely hint of orange.

Gingersnaps

1 Lightly grease several cookie sheets with a little butter.

2 Sift the flour, salt, sugar, ginger, and baking soda into a large bowl.

3 Heat the butter and light corn syrup together in a pan over very low heat until the butter has melted.

4 Remove the pan from the heat and let the butter mixture cool slightly, then pour it onto the dry ingredients.

5 Add the egg and orange peel and mix well to form a dough.

6 Using your hands, carefully shape the dough into 30 even-size balls.

7 Place the dough balls well apart on the prepared cookie sheets, then flatten them slightly with your fingers.

8 Bake in a preheated oven, 325°F/160°C, for 15–20 minutes, then carefully transfer the cookies to a wire rack to cool and crispen before serving.

MAKES 30 COOKIES

½ cup butter, plus extra for greasing
2½ cups self-rising flour
pinch of salt
1 cup superfine sugar
1 tbsp ground ginger
1 tsp baking soda
¼ cup light corn syrup
1 egg, beaten lightly
1 tsp grated orange peel

NUTRITION
Calories *106*; Sugars *9 g*; Protein *1 g*; Carbohydrate *18 g*; Fat *4 g*; Saturates *2 g*

⭐⭐⭐   moderate
🕐   10 mins
🕐   20 mins

COOK'S TIP

Store these cookies in an airtight container and eat them within 1 week.

These crunchy cookies will be popular with children of all ages as they contain their favorite food—peanut butter.

Peanut Butter Cookies

MAKES 20 COOKIES

½ cup butter, softened, plus extra
   for greasing
½ cup chunky peanut butter
generous 1 cup granulated sugar
1 egg, beaten lightly
generous 1 cup all-purpose flour
½ tsp baking powder
pinch of salt
½ cup chopped unsalted natural peanuts

1 Lightly grease 2 cookie sheets with a little butter.

2 Beat the butter and peanut butter together in a large bowl.

3 Gradually add the granulated sugar and beat well.

4 Add the beaten egg, a little at a time, beating well after each addition until it is well blended.

5 Sift the flour, baking powder, and salt into the peanut butter mixture.

6 Add the chopped peanuts and mix to form a soft dough. Wrap in plastic wrap and let chill in the refrigerator for 30 minutes.

7 Shape the dough into 20 balls and place them on the prepared cookie sheets about 2 inches/5 cm apart to allow for spreading during cooking. Flatten them slightly with your hand.

8 Bake in a preheated oven, 375°F/190°C, for 15 minutes or until golden-brown. Transfer the cookies to a wire rack and let cool.

NUTRITION
Calories *186*; Sugars *13 g*; Protein *4 g*;
Carbohydrate *19 g*; Fat *11 g*; Saturates *5 g*

⭐⭐   easy

🌀   40 mins

🕐   15 mins

 COOK'S TIP

For a crunchy bite and sparkling appearance, sprinkle the cookies with raw brown sugar before baking.

These oaty, fruity cookies are delicious with a cup of coffee for a special reward after a busy morning.

Oat *and* Raisin Cookies

1 Lightly grease 2 cookie sheets with a little butter.

2 Cream the butter and sugar together in a large bowl until light and fluffy.

3 Gradually add the beaten egg, beating well after each addition until thoroughly blended.

4 Sift the flour, salt, and baking powder together into the creamed mixture. Mix well. Add the oats, raisins, and sesame seeds, and mix to form a dough.

5 Place spoonfuls of the mixture spaced well apart on the prepared cookie sheets to allow room for expansion during cooking. Flatten them slightly with the back of a spoon.

6 Bake in a preheated oven, 350°F/180°C, for 15 minutes.

7 Remove the cookies from the oven and let cool for a few minutes on the cookie sheets. Carefully transfer the cookies to a wire rack and let cool completely before serving.

MAKES 10 COOKIES

4 tbsp butter, plus extra for greasing
generous ½ cup superfine sugar
1 egg, beaten lightly
generous ⅓ cup all-purpose flour
½ tsp salt
½ tsp baking powder
2 cups rolled oats
¾ cup raisins
2 tbsp sesame seeds

NUTRITION

Calories *227*; Sugars *22 g*; Protein *4 g*; Carbohydrate *39 g*; Fat *7 g*; Saturates *3 g*

⭐⭐ easy

🕐 50 mins

🕐 15 mins

COOK'S TIP

To enjoy these cookies at their best, store them in an airtight container.

For a sweet treat, try these pretty crescent-shaped cookies, which have a lovely citrus tang to them.

Citrus Crescents

MAKES 25 COOKIES

⅓ cup butter, softened, plus extra for greasing
⅓ cup superfine sugar, plus extra for sprinkling (optional)
1 egg, separated
scant 1½ cups all-purpose flour, plus extra for dusting
grated zest of 1 orange
grated zest of 1 lemon
grated zest of 1 lime
2–3 tbsp orange juice

1 Lightly grease 2 cookie sheets with a little butter.

2 Cream the butter and sugar together in a large bowl until light and fluffy, then gradually beat in the egg yolk.

3 Sift the flour into the creamed mixture and mix until blended. Add the citrus zests to the mixture, with enough orange juice to form a soft dough.

4 Roll out the dough on a lightly floured surface. Stamp out circles, using a 3-inch/7.5-cm cookie cutter. Make crescent shapes by cutting away a quarter of each circle. Re-roll the trimmings to make about 25 crescents.

5 Place the crescents on the prepared cookie sheets, spacing them well apart to allow room for expansion during cooking. Prick the surface of each crescent with a fork.

6 Lightly whisk the egg white in a small bowl and brush it over the cookies. Dust with extra superfine sugar, if using.

7 Bake in a preheated oven, 400°F/200°C, for 12–15 minutes. Carefully transfer the cookies to a wire rack and let cool and crispen before serving.

NUTRITION
Calories 72; Sugars 3 g; Protein 1 g;
Carbohydrate 10 g; Fat 4 g; Saturates 2 g

⭐⭐⭐   moderate

🖐   10 mins

🕐   15 mins

 COOK'S TIP

Store the citrus crescents in an airtight container. Alternatively, they can be frozen for up to 1 month.

These cookies are perfect for afternoon tea or they can be served with vanilla ice cream for a really delicious dessert.

Shortbread Fantails

1 Lightly grease a shallow 8-inch/20-cm round cake pan with a little butter.

2 Cream the butter, the granulated sugar, and the confectioners' sugar together in a large bowl until light and fluffy.

3 Sift the flour and salt into the creamed mixture. Add the orange flower water and mix to form a soft dough.

4 Roll out the dough on a lightly floured surface to an 8-inch/20-cm circle and place in the prepared pan. Prick the dough well and score into 8 triangles with a round-bladed knife.

5 Bake the shortbread in a preheated oven, 300°F/150°C, for 30–35 minutes or until crisp and a pale golden color.

6 Remove from the oven and sprinkle with superfine sugar, then cut along the marked lines to make the 8 fantails.

7 Let cool in the pan. Store in an airtight container.

SERVES 8

½ cup butter, softened, plus extra for greasing
scant ¼ cup granulated sugar
2 tbsp confectioners' sugar
generous 1½ cups all-purpose flour, plus extra for dusting
pinch of salt
2 tsp orange flower water
superfine sugar, for sprinkling

NUTRITION
Calories *248*; Sugars *10 g*; Protein *3 g*; Carbohydrate *32 g*; Fat *13 g*; Saturates *9 g*

⭐⭐ easy
🖐 40 mins
🕐 35 mins

COOK'S TIP

For a crunchy addition, sprinkle 2 tablespoons of chopped mixed nuts over the top of the fantails before baking.

These rock drops are more substantial than a crisp cookie. Serve them fresh from the oven to enjoy them at their best.

Rock Drops

MAKES 8 COOKIES

⅓ cup butter, cut into small pieces, plus
    extra for greasing
scant 1½ cups all-purpose flour
2 tsp baking powder
⅓ cup raw brown sugar
½ cup golden raisins
2 tbsp candied cherries, chopped finely
1 egg, beaten lightly
2 tbsp milk

1 Lightly grease a cookie sheet with a little butter.

2 Sift the flour and baking powder into a large bowl. Add the butter and rub in with your fingertips until the mixture resembles bread crumbs.

3 Stir in the raw brown sugar, golden raisins, and candied cherries.

4 Add the beaten egg and milk to the mixture and mix to form a soft dough.

5 Spoon 8 mounds of the mixture onto the prepared cookie sheet, spacing them well apart to allow for expansion during cooking.

6 Bake in a preheated oven, 400°F/200°C, for about 15–20 minutes or until firm to the touch when pressed with a finger.

7 Remove the rock drops from the cookie sheet. Either serve piping hot from the oven or transfer to a wire rack and let cool before serving.

NUTRITION
Calories *270*; Sugars *21 g*; Protein *4 g*;
Carbohydrate *41 g*; Fat *11 g*; Saturates *7 g*

easy

5–10 mins

20 mins

🧑‍🍳 **COOK'S TIP**

For convenience, prepare the dry ingredients in advance and stir in the liquid just before cooking.

These are just as meringues should be— as light as air and at the same time crisp and melt-in-the-mouth.

Meringues

1 Line 3 cookie sheets with sheets of baking parchment.

2 Using an electric hand-held whisk or a balloon whisk, whisk the egg whites with a pinch of salt in a large clean bowl until stiff. You should be able to turn the bowl upside down without any movement from the egg whites.

3 Whisk in the granulated sugar, a little at a time; the meringue should start to look glossy at this stage.

4 Sprinkle in the superfine sugar, a little at a time, and whisk until the sugar has been incorporated and the meringue is thick, white, and stands in tall peaks.

5 Transfer the meringue mixture to a pastry bag fitted with a 3/4-inch/2-cm star tip. Pipe about 26 small whirls onto the prepared cookie sheets.

6 Bake in a preheated oven, 250°F/120°C, for 1½ hours or until the meringues are pale golden in color and can be easily lifted off the parchment. Let cool in the turned-off oven overnight.

7 Just before serving, sandwich the meringues together in pairs with the whipped cream and arrange on a serving plate.

MAKES 13 MERINGUES

4 egg whites
2/3 cup granulated sugar
2/3 cup superfine sugar
salt
1 cup heavy cream, whipped lightly, to serve

NUTRITION
Calories *183*; Sugars *21 g*; Protein *1 g*; Carbohydrate *21 g*; Fat *11 g*; Saturates *7 g*

⭐⭐ easy
🕐 15 mins
🕐 1 hr 30 mins

🍳 **COOK'S TIP**

For a finer texture, replace the granulated sugar with superfine sugar.

Index